AF888745

Awaken My Inner Zen

365 Inspirations to Help Teens Develop Inner Calm, Life Balance, and Mindfulness

LLH Publishing

Published and Distributed in Canada by LLH Publishing Inc.
www.andreaseydel.com

Library of Congress Cataloging-in-Publication Data

Seydel, Andrea
Awaken My Inner Zen: 365 Inspirations to Help Teens Develop Inner Calm, Life Balance, and Mindfulness \ Andrea Seydel
1.Juvenile Nonfiction-Health & Daily Living -2. Non Fiction-Self-Help-Motivation & Inspiration
ISBN- 978-0-9812598-9-5
1st Printing: December 2018. Printed in Canada

Cover Photo Credit: Katie Burkhart (Rocks)
Proofreader: Lindy Bailey

Publisher's Note & Author DISCLAIMER
This publication is designed to provide accurate and authoritative information concerning the subject matter covered. It is sold with the understanding that the publisher and author is not engaging in or rendering any psychological, medical or other professional services. If expert assistance or counseling is needed, seek the services of a competent medical professional. For immediate support call your local crisis line.
BE WELL.

To my Mom, Carole, for having such a warm way of comforting and calming! For teaching me how to "talk to myself," and for continuously reassuring me that things will get better during life challenges.
I love you beyond words!!

Awaken My Inner Zen

One Day at a Time

January 1

Hold comfort in your heart

"Whatever you're facing right now,
there's a way out."
Paul Jukes

Today's message...

Take comfort knowing you are strong
and do what brings comfort to your heart.
Put your mind at ease.

Remember...

Sometimes it is important to remind yourself
that everything will be ok.
Writing in a journal is a way of talking to yourself
without being interrupted.
Find things that bring you comfort
and do them during your times of struggle.

Ask yourself...

What brings me peace?
What brings me mental clarity?
What brings me comfort?

January 2

Take notice of friendship

***"The greatest healing therapy
is friendship and love."***
Hubert Humphrey

Today's message...

Think about all the things that are going well
for you right now, and notice all
the love that surrounds you.
It is up to you to believe
good things are on their way
and happening for you on their own time.
Take the moments that you are in
and make them meaningful;
trust that patience and faith
will pay off for you.

Ask yourself...

Who are my good friends?
How can I rebuild myself?
Who helps and supports me along my path?

January 3

Enjoy gentle environments

"There is nothing like staying at home for real comfort."
Jane Austen

Remember...

Gentle people often treat others with
kindness and a mild manner; you will need
these people at certain times in your life.
Be kind to yourself and learn to love
who and what you are, forgive yourself.
Retrain your mind to seek peace regularly.
Surround yourself with warm
and caring people and things.
Notice the people in your environment!

Affirm...

I choose gentleness and peace in my life.
I listen to beautiful calming music.
I surround myself with beauty and calm.

January 4

Choose to find peace

***"Forgive others,
not because they
deserve forgiveness,
but because you
deserve peace."***
Jonathan Lockwood Huie

Today's message...

Peace is the end result of training and re-training
your mind to interpret life as it is
rather than how you think it should be.
Don't let the bad behaviour of others
destroy your sense of inner peace.
Live in the moment and trust in harmony.
Take a deep breath and respect yourself enough
to say, "I deserve peace."

Ask yourself...

How can I stop fighting and go with the flow, and
in doing so, find peace?
Can I be selective in my battles?
Is proving I am right more important than my peace?

January 5

Be understanding with yourself

"Don't just be good to others.
Be good to yourself too."
Old Saying

Today's message...

You deserve to have all the wonderful things in life.
It's ok to focus on self-care and be a bit selfish.
Taking time to yourself will help you grow and learn.
Nobody in life is perfect, it's important
not to be hard on yourself.
Accept exactly who you are,
and be grateful for the life you are living.

Ask yourself...

How can I love myself unconditionally?
What standards am I setting?
What am I most thankful for in my life?

January 6

Trust that all is well

"It's not the load that brings you down, it's the way you carry it."
Lou Holtz

Remember...

Surrendering isn't about being passive,
but it is about being open to
possibilities beyond your control.
Release the stress in your life
by learning to let go of the things
you cannot control or change.
Your thoughts are powerful;
be careful what you think about.
Sometimes you have to stop
worrying, wondering, and controlling,
and have faith that things will all work out.

Affirm...

I no longer allow negative thoughts to drain my energy.
I let go and make room for something better.
All is well and I notice the good in my life.

January 7

Notice and embrace miracles

***"Be faithful in small things because
it is in them that your peace lies."***
Mother Teresa

Today's message...

Miracles will start happening for you when
you give just as much effort towards
your dreams as you do your worries.
Look for the gifts and the miracles (big and small)
that happen each and every day for you.
Life is full of beauty,
but you will only notice it
if you are looking for it,
everyday.

Ask yourself...

How can I graciously notice the magical blessings
from the world around me?
What am I most grateful for?
Do I notice the abundance around me?
How can I change my expectations
and appreciate everything?

January 8

Trust you are exactly where you need to be

"Stress makes you believe that everything has to happen right now. Faith reassures you that everything will happen in good time."
Unknown

Remember...

Faith is like taking the first step across
a scary bridge when you can't see the other side.
Stress and pressure appear when you think
you have to figure every thing out,
but life has a funny way of working out in the end.
No need to stress!

Affirm...

I believe in myself.
I have faith things will work out well for me.
I am patient and trust everything will work out fine.

January 9

Find your inner power

***"Smile and let everyone know that today,
you're a lot stronger than
you were yesterday."***
Drake

Today's message...

You are much stronger than you think that you are.
The struggles that you are exposed to in your life
are developing the strength for what you need
tomorrow and the next day.
When you feel like you can't go any further,
just know that you have plenty of power within you,
and the strength that led you this far
has the ability to carry you even further.

Ask yourself...

How can I believe in myself a little more?
How can I stay positive, even when
I feel like my life is falling apart?
What are my strengths?

January 10

Everything will fall into place

"Relax. Don't worry.
Everything's going to be alright."
Old Saying

Remember...

Allow your life to unfold as naturally as possible
and trust that everything will fall into place.
It isn't "who you are" that can hold you back,
but rather "who you think you are not"
that hinders your life.
Start your day positively
and monitor your thinking.

Affirm...

I appreciate all the good in my life.
I let go of worry and pressure.
Everything is good and falls into place.

January 11

Open your heart

"If there is anything better than to be loved, it is loving."
Anne Frank

Today's message...

Take time to show love to the people who are regularly there for you and support you even through tough times.
Be loving towards yourself and other people, you will be surprised how good it feels.
It is a true statement that you never truly know what someone is going through, you could be a little sunshine in what could feel like darkness in their life.

Ask yourself...

How can I be kind and loving to someone in my life today?
Can I think of the most challenging people in my life and notice that these are the ones that need extra love?
How can I be loving and kind to others and myself?

January 12

Notice if you're exaggerating fears

"If you want to conquer fear,
don't sit home and think about it.
Go out and get busy."
Dale Carnegie

Remember...

When you despair you remember all the things
that are going wrong or bad in your life.
Reroute your thinking back
to hope and positivity.
Fear is simply a feeling, and feelings can be changed.
When you focus on problems,
you will see more problems;
when you focus on possibilities,
you will have more opportunities.

Affirm...

I let go of fear.
I choose to see opportunity.
I reroute my thinking and choose hope.

January 13

Take responsibility

"The moment you take responsibility for everything in your life is the moment you can change anything in you life."
Hal Elrod

Remember...

You sometimes need a great deal of courage to
let go of the things or people in your life
that no longer serve you well.
Take a stand about the things in
your life that really matter.
Ask yourself daily what is
really important to you,
and then find the courage
to build it into your life.

Affirm...

I take personal responsibility for my life.
I am courageous.
I take a stand for what is important to me.

January 14

Be gentle with yourself and others

"A kind gesture can reach a wound that only compassion can heal!"
Dr. Steve Maraboli

Remember...

Love and appreciate people around you exactly as they are.
Give yourself and others the gift of unconditional love and acceptance.
Be gentle with yourself, and learn to love and to forgive yourself.
There is no need to strive for perfection, be your own best friend.

Affirm...

I choose to act with compassion.
I accept myself unconditionally.
I am my own best friend.

January 15

Have willingness to be free

"Stop letting it bother you,
just let it go."
Old Saying

Today's message...

Stop letting things hang over you
and keep bringing you down.
Be willing to let go of the things that bother you,
and find courage to let go of the things you can't change.
Know when you need to release
old anger and frustration.
Save and give the best part of who you are
to the people who really deserve
to have you in their life.

Ask yourself...

Can I let go of anyone in my life that does not feel happy?
What changes can I make in my life that will
let go of any toxic people?
What generous and kind people can
I welcome into my life?

January 16

Surround yourself with positive people and situations

"Surround yourself with positive energy."
Jackie Mannell

Today's message...

One positive thought could override
a day that is going bad.
Stay close to anything and everything that
makes you feel like you are thrilled to be alive.
There are no regrets or reasons
to dwell on negative situations,
just learn lessons and move forward.

Ask yourself...

How can I no longer allow negative thoughts
or feelings to drain my energy?
How can I focus on the good that is in my life?
How can I be responsible for the energy that I bring?

January 17

Set positive intentions

"Wake up, smile, and tell yourself: today is my day!"
Old Saying

Today's message...

Set the tone for the day by expecting wonderful things to happen during the day.
Express gratitude first thing in the morning.
When you wake up take a long, deep breath and smile because you are alive.
Worry is a waste of time;
good and bad things will always happen in your life, but you just have to keep focusing on the good things and stay positive.

Ask yourself...

Can I give forgive for yesterday's mistakes, and focus on positive thoughts?
Who in my life lifts me higher and has good intentions?
How can I attract good things into my life?

January 18

Awaken to your world

"The past is your lesson.
The present is your gift.
The future is your motivation."
Zig Ziglar

Today's message...

Concentrate and focus on the world
around you and embrace its beauty.
Train your mind to see positive in every situation
and you will experience your world positively.
Start believing today that things are going
to change for the better.
You have exciting wonderful things
coming to you in the future.

Ask yourself...

What positive thought can finish my day?
What is something important that I can do today?
What memory can I make for tomorrow?

January 19

You are strong

"Put the worst behind you
so the best can find you."
Billy Cox

Today's message...

Problems and challenges are inevitable in your life.
Reaching obstacles could stop you,
but the worst is behind you and you are
capable of overcoming challenge.
Trial and suffering can be the fuel to strengthen
ambition and inspiration,
and help you to achieve great things.

Ask yourself...

How have I overcome difficulties in the past?
How can I choose to be a warrior during challenge?
How can I decide to be strong and not be a victim
of the circumstances?

January 20

Reclaim your passion

"Sometimes life is about risking everything for a dream no one can see but you."
Unknown

Remember...

Allow yourself to be and do all the things
you are meant to do and be.
Stop expecting others to do
what you can do for yourself;
take back ownership of your life
and regain your own self-respect.
Follow your passion and you will create
a future full of play, purpose, and success.
Take back your power today!

Affirm...

I take back my power.
I reclaim the passion inside me.
I am responsible for my life.

January 21

Clear your inner house

"Sometimes your heart needs more time to accept what your mind already knows."
Old Saying

Remember...

Let your past relationships
make you better and not bitter.
Take all the time you need to heal emotionally
and release any blocks to healing.
Let go of the people and things that hurt you,
but never forget what lessons they taught you.

Affirm...

I release toxic people from my life.
I let go of hurt and mend my broken heart.
I forgive and focus forward.

January 22

See the bright side of things

"When things go wrong,
don't go with them."
Elvis Presley

Remember...

Look beyond imperfections
and keep an eye out for opportunities.
Your words and attitude carry amazing power
over yourself and others around you.
Try to stay in a place of noticing and observing,
instead of judging and criticizing.
When you speak, try to uplift others.

Affirm...

I am positive.
I look for opportunities.
I see the bright side of things.

January 23

Be gentle

"Your calm mind is
the ultimate weapon
against challenges.
So relax."
Bryant McGill

Today's message...

Set aside at least one hour every day for personal development and renewal. This powerful strategy allows you to be gentle on yourself and reflect. Be gentle with yourself, chances are that you are doing your very best.

Ask yourself...

Where do I find peace amongst all chaos in my life?
Do I overthink things and end up creating problems that weren't even there?
How can I be gentle with myself?

January 24

Open your mind

"Being happy doesn't mean that everything is perfect. It means that you've decided to look beyond the imperfections."
Gerard Way

Today's message...

Compromise is about deciding that the other person has an equal amount of the right to be happy as you do. Life and people are not always perfect, but situations will be what you make of them. Relationships will consist of ups and downs, you are meant to ride through all the challenges while learning and growing.

Ask yourself...

How have I compromised in the past?
How can I broaden my perspective and see things in my life as perfectly imperfect?
How can I listen to others to understand their point of view?

January 25

Listen to your inner voice

***"There is a voice that doesn't use words.
Listen."***
Rumi

Today's message...

Give yourself permission to walk away from
anything that gives you a bad feeling.
Your inner voice needs to be heard when it speaks.
Listen to positive people and ignore the negative
people that doubt, judge, or criticize.
It's ok to have negative thoughts,
just don't let negative thinking take control.
Listen to what your gut is telling you today!

Ask yourself...

Do other people's opinions drown out my own inner voice?
There is a voice inside me that is whispering to me
all day long: what is it saying?
How can I pay attention to my inner voice
and avoid overriding what it's saying?

January 26

Relax and take a deep breath

"If you want to be happy,
you have to be happy
on purpose."
Joel Osteen

Today's message...

Sometimes, it's hard to pick right from wrong. The best thing you can do is go with all your heart, take a deep breath, and hope it all goes well. You may not be okay right now, but it will all be ok. Soon, when you look back on challenging periods in your life, you are going to be so glad you never gave up. Be happy on purpose today because you decided to be happy!

Affirm...

All is well.
I am ok.
I am going to make it.

January 27

Go have some fun

"Find some beautiful place to get lost."
Elliott Smith

Remember...

You can't always play it safe.
In the end you will only regret the chances
and opportunities that you didn't take.
Take risks and fully experience your life.
Don't be afraid of experience,
because the more experience you have,
the more mature and happy you become.

Affirm...

I am trying something new.
I am awake and alive.
I get lost in my experiences.

January 28

Do what brings you comfort

"Set peace of mind as your highest goal, and organize your life around it."
Brian Tracy

Today's message...

Think about the things that make you feel good.
What has helped you to feel comfort in the past?
Try to make a list of all the things you enjoy,
so that when you are in need of comfort
you can draw on this list.
Whether it's a nice bath, a walk in nature,
or simply reading a good book,
when you need peace and comfort,
you will know what to do.

Ask yourself...

What warms my heart?
What activities make me feel good?
When I need comforting, who can I talk to?

January 29

Connect to your playful self

"Can your inner child come out and play?"
David Icke

Today's message...

You are meant to enjoy life
and do the things that bring you pleasure.
Go out with your friends
or plan something different than
you would typically do.
It does not matter how old you are,
there is an inner child within you
that seeks fun and laughter.
Re-evaluate how you spend your time;
enjoy quality time with your family and friends.

Ask yourself...

How can I love and nurture the part of me
that is my inner child?
What child-like wonder can I surround myself with?
How can I look at the world with child-like fearlessness?

January 30

Enjoy the moment

***"Life is a gift.
Never forget to enjoy
and bask in every
moment you are in."***
Celestine Chua

Remember...

Turn inward and learn from your inner voice
and you will see the world more clearly.
Being mindful allows magic to flow into your life.
In each moment you receive clues and gifts
that guide you for your future.
Enjoy the moments today!

Affirm...

I celebrate my life and enjoy this moment.
I train my brain to see positive.
I see clearly and I am present in the moment.

January 31

Leave behind what isn't serving you

"Stop focusing on how stressed you are and remember how blessed you are."
Gautama Buddha

Today's message...

Every trial and challenge in life has
a hidden blessing or gift.
Let go or leave behind the things in life
that are not positively serving you.
If you don't like something, welcome positive change.
Challenge can bring about new opportunities,
so be sure to stay optimistic.

Ask yourself...

What part of my life is turning upside down?
What would happen if I look at things differently
and welcome positive change?
How can I let go of the things that are not
helping me to flourish?

February 1

A new beginning

"Everyday is a new beginning,
take a deep breath and start again."
Ritu Ghatourey

Today's message...

Approach life as if it is a continual stream of new beginnings. Make space in your life for new wonderful things to arrive. The joy of life comes from new opportunities and experiences. Keep growing and changing, let go of old things that don't serve you any longer.

Ask yourself...

Am I open to whatever is coming next?
How can I stretch my mind today?
What do I believe will come my way?

February 2

Avoid thinking about what you don't want

"Watch your thoughts, they become words.
Watch your words, they become actions.
Watch your actions, they become habits."
Winston Churchill

Today's message...

Be careful how you think because
your thoughts are very powerful.
What you think about yourself
and your own perspective
is much more meaningful and important
than what anyone else may think of you.
Use the power of your mind to manifest
what you desire for yourself in your life.
You can mentally prepare for the life you desire.

Ask yourself...

My mind is a powerful thing; how can I
fill it with positive thoughts?
What would it be like to practice happy thinking everyday?
If I allow myself to dream, what is my ideal life and what
action can I towards it take every day?

February 3

Everything has perfect timing

"Take life day by day and be grateful for the little things. Don't get stressed over what you can't control."
Unknown

Remember...

Be in love with your life and the loving people
that you already have in it.
It's during this time life feels so much brighter.
If you keep on moving forward while
taking notice of the gifts around you,
everything will come to you at the right time.
Trust that everything will show up at the perfect time.
Enjoy the moments you are in today.

Affirm...

I have faith all will work out well.
I appreciate the love and support around me.
Good things are unfolding in my life.

February 4

Remain positive and keep dreaming

"Stay positive even when it feels like your whole world is falling apart."
Old Saying

Today's message...

Keep your head up and stay positive.
The tough challenges you face
will help you grow and learn.
No matter how much things can hurt
in current situations, one day you will look back on
challenges and realize those times have
changed your life for the better.
Good things will come to you
when you believe that
better things are coming.

Ask yourself...

How can I stay positive, work harder,
and make things happen?
How can I shift my focus to what really matters
and stay positive?
Good things happen when I least expect it;
how can I keep moving forward?

February 5

Take a break from negativity

"The less you respond to negative people, the more peaceful your life will become."
Unknown

Remember...

When you are positive and grateful,
you send out good energy and wonderful
things will be attracted into your life.
Whatever is bringing you down,
try to get rid of it as fast as possible
so you don't have negativity in your life.
Never underestimate the power of a positive
explanatory style of thinking and acting.

Affirm...

Today, I choose to focus on good things.
Negative energy is not welcome here.
I think positively and abundantly.

February 6

Nurture your dreams

"Have patience.
Everything is difficult
before it is easy."
Saadi Shirazi

Today's message...

Have faith that the seeds you have planted
in your life will start to grow.
Every thing in life that is worth having takes
time, nurturing, and care in order to grow.
When something is not working for you,
be patient and trust that it will work
if it is supposed to.
Give your dreams a chance to grow!

Ask yourself...

What can I nurture in my life?
How can I step back and allow each moment to bring joy?
When can I take time for my own development?

February 7

Release

"Saying yes to happiness means learning to say no to the things and people that stress you out."
Thema Davis

Today's message...

There are going to be things and people
in your life that do not feel good.
It is important to let go of situations
that are out of your control.
Also, choose the quality of people
you spend your time with.
Let joy be your magnet;
in other words go to the things that
bring you happiness and joy.
Move away from, or release, the things
that cause discontent or stress.

Ask yourself...

Who in my life brings me
a sense of peace and support?
What needs to be minimized?
What can I choose to let go of?

February 8

Have faith in yourself

"Your faith can move mountains and your doubt can create them."
Old Saying

Today's message...

Faith is about believing you don't know what
will be happening in your life,
but you know that things will happen
and it will all work out fine.
You can't control everything
that happens in your life
and you can't control the future,
but you can relax and have faith
that all things will work out.
If you believe in yourself and your abilities,
anything is possible for you.

Ask yourself...

Have I had any challenges in my life that have
led to wonderful outcomes?
What dreams do I want to follow?
How can I believe in myself a little more?

February 9

Find your inner power

"Beautiful things happen in your life when you distance yourself from the negative things."
Zig Ziglar

Remember...

Strength shows up in your ability to persist and continue even amongst challenges. Never underestimate your ability to change yourself and bring inner strength. Strength and growth come from the continual exposure to effort, persistence, and challenge.

Affirm...

My inner power is beautiful.
I am strong and powerful.
I spread inner peace.

February 10

Move into gratitude and appreciation

"The happiest people don't have the best of everything, they just make the best of everything."
Unknown

Today's message...

Just go with the flow and force nothing, it feels much easier. Eventually all the pieces of your life puzzle will fall into place. Trust that all the pieces will reveal themselves at the perfect time. Keep yourself occupied with positive thoughts and gratitude.

Ask yourself...

How can I catch myself being negative or self-critical?
Would I say negative things to my child or friend?
How can I work on myself, by myself, and for myself?

February 11

Stop dwelling on problems

***"As you waste your energy
complaining about life,
someone out there
is struggling to breathe.
Appreciate what you have.
Be thankful and stop complaining."***
Unknown

Today's message...

Shift your focus from focusing on problems or challenges to focusing on things you are grateful for in your life. If you catch yourself dwelling on problems, make a mental switch towards appreciation of what is good.

Affirm...

I am grateful for the good in my life.
My life is full of gifts.
I put my energy on appreciating life.

February 12

Release worry and fear

"When you expect the best you release a magnetic force in your mind which, by the law of attraction, tends to bring the best to you."
Norman Vincent Peale

Today's message...

Hope for the best and begin to expect only good things coming to you from any situation. You can conquer any fear but you have to make up your mind to do so. Negative thoughts can destroy you; change your thinking towards noticing more positive.

Ask yourself...

Can I take my mind off of troubles and get my mind to focus on my needs?
When has my thinking been negative?
Can I look for the positive in everything?

February 13

Be mindful

"Sometimes you will never know the true value of a moment until it becomes a memory."

Dr. Seuss

Today's message...

Even when things seem like
they are really dark or terrible,
the darkness will end and give
way to brightness and good.
Sometimes having things not go
the way you want is
a wonderful stroke of luck.
Express emotions and let go of hurt.
There is power in finding the beauty in
the challenging things that happen to you.

Ask yourself...

Maybe it is not a good day today, but how is it alright?
What learning is inside my pain and disappointment?
What pain do I need to let go of?

February 14

It's time to unburden your pain

"When someone treats you like crap just remember it's because there's something wrong with them, not you."
Karen Salmansohn

Remember...

Sadness is only a temporary experience,
and it will pass.
Be ok with your uneasiness,
as it is a sign that you are human.
Choose to see your challenges as hidden blessings
and expect good things to come from difficult situations.
The past is where you learn your lessons;
you can use these lessons and apply them in the future.
Keep in mind the pain that you feel might be
a result of someone else's issues,
not yours.

Affirm...

I am ready to grow and learn.
I let go of past hurt and pain.
I acknowledge my sadness and focus forward.

February 15

Nourish and blossom

"Every beautiful butterfly was once a dreary caterpillar."
Old Saying

Remember...

Each day is an opportunity to blossom
and emerge into your beautiful life.
Change is a process of growing into
the special person you were meant to be.
Take time to grow, learn, and evolve.
If you get better and you
see success as a result,
use that as motivation
to keep getting better.

Affirm...

I am getting better everyday.
Things are emerging for me.
I nourish myself and grow everyday.

February 16

Listen to your intuition

"Once you make a decision,
the universe conspires
to make it happen."
Ralph Waldo Emerson

Today's message...

Make a decision, and don't look back.
Sometimes it is the smallest decisions
that can change your life.
It is time to take charge.
Don't base your decision on
the advice of other people;
they do not have to deal with
the consequence of the decision.

Ask yourself...

What is my intuition saying to me?
I am in control: how can I take charge of my own life?
What decisions do I need to make?

February 17

Look for hidden blessings everywhere

***"Keep the smile, leave the tension,
feel the joy, forget the worry,
hold the peace, leave pain,
and always be happy."***
Unknown

Remember...

Everything comes to an eventual ending.
Make peace with the fact that you don't have to worry,
that everything will be ok for you.
Sometimes all you need to do
is take a deep cleansing breath.
Pick yourself up and trust that everything is
happening the way it is supposed to for you.

Ask yourself...

What do I worry about?
Can I think of any hidden blessings in my life?
What blessings are surrounding me?

February 18

Notice the treasures in your life

"If you look the right way, you can see the whole world is a garden."
Frances Hodgson Burnett

Today's message...

Embrace your life and count your blessings.
Own your own story and love yourself
through the process.
All your needs are continuously met
and anything is possible for you.
Raise your standards for your life
and your needs will be met.
Appreciate what you already have and watch
your prosperity and wealth increase.

Ask yourself...

How can I embrace who I am,
and not apologize for being me?
Can I see prosperity in my life?
Where are my opportunities, ideas, and support?

February 19

Be careful with your thinking

"Whatever you believe about yourself on the inside is what you will **manifest on the outside."**
Mahatma Gandhi

Remember...

Pay close attention to your thinking today.
Notice the inner critic or negative voice taking over.
What we repeat over and over become strong messages.
Rethink your thinking.

Affirm...

Today, I am careful with my thinking.
I train my brain to be nice to me.
I create a positive world with my thinking.

February 20

Love yourself more

"What if you simply devoted this day to loving yourself more?"
Unknown

Remember...

Try and remember the things
that make you happy.
What makes you happy that you could
add into your day?
You show you are a loving person by
honouring what brings you joy!

Ask yourself...

What makes me feel good?
What makes me feel loved?
How can I love myself more today?

February 21

Run your own race

"No matter what, just do you."
Expression

Today's message...

Everyone has his or her own lane,
maintain yours and you will notice it feels more
comfortable to focus on yourself.
A flower does not compete with the flower
next to it because they all bloom
and are uniquely beautiful.
Use others as inspiration towards
your own unique mission.
Don't let it bring you down.

Ask yourself...

How can I stay focused on my own life?
What makes me powerful?
How can I just do me?

February 22

Allow yourself to emerge

***"Take a deep breath.
It's just a bad day,
not a bad life."***
Old Saying

Today's message...

Every now and then there is a new you that emerges.
It is still made up of you at the core,
but a bright, fresh, and renewed version of you.
You have reinvented a better version of yourself
that is not afraid, has personal boundaries,
and sprouts strongly out into the world.
You are getting better, stronger, and wiser everyday.

Ask yourself...

What seeds do I want to plant today for future growth?
What aspects of my life keep getting better?
How can I keep working on myself and trust
everything will blossom?

February 23

Learning opportunity

"Failure is only the opportunity to begin again, only this time more wisely."
Henry Ford

Remember...

Don't be too hard on yourself.
Look at everything as an opportunity
to learn something new.
Learn from your experiences
and use them in a positive way.

Ask yourself...

What lessons have I learned?
What can I take away from this?
How do I explain this to myself?

February 24

You're ok

"Everything will be ok."
Old Saying

Today's message...

Everything will be good soon.
Just hang in there and don't worry
yourself about it too much.
Tough times don't last.
Look for things you can
appreciate and be grateful for
around you today to shift your energy.

Affirm...

Today is a new day.
I am ok.
It's ok to be just ok.

February 25

Look at your routines

"To change your life,
you need to change
your priorities."
John C. Maxwell

Today's message...

In order to establish what takes priority in your life, you have to be willing to say no to something else. Take time to step back and examine what's really important to you in life. Make that your priority. When you let go, you are making space and room for something even bigger and better.

Ask yourself...

What are my priorities?
Can I remove commitments that do not bring me happiness?
What needs my attention now?

February 26

Claim your power

Ask yourself...

How can I take responsibility of my life?
What are my unique gifts and talents?
How can I flex the muscle of courage?

Remember...

Shift your perspective to being in control
instead of being controlled.
The most common way that someone loses
their power is that they think they don't have any.
Distance yourself from the world
and connect again with your own voice.

Affirm...

I believe in myself.
I let go of limiting beliefs.
I reclaim my power and express my strengths.

February 27

You have what you need within

"Life has many ways of testing a person's will, either by having nothing happen at all or by having everything happen all at once."
Paulo Coelho

Remember...

Vision is the ability to see potential
in what others overlook.
A true tragedy in your life would be
to let your talent die inside you.
Awaken to your potential today.
Only put blinders on to block those things
that conspire to hold you back.
See that all that you need is within you.

Affirm...

I look for magic in my daily routine.
I wake up to my life.
I am full of potential.

February 28

Find your own happy place

"Anything that gets your blood racing is probably worth doing."
Hunter Thompson

Today's message...

When you have great passion
you can make anything happen.
Discover YOU and find your own
passion and life purpose.
Your passion will eventually lead you to your purpose.
Whatever your mind can think of, dream of,
or conceive, you can achieve.
Get clues from the things that excite you!

Ask yourself...

What excites me and makes me feel enthusiastic?
What is really important?
What is my burning desire?

February 29
(Bonus/Leap Year)

Be optimistic and stay determined

"Optimism is a happiness magnet.
If you stay positive,
good things and good people
will be drawn to you."
Mary Lou Retton

Remember...

Keep going so you can be successful;
make mistakes, but don't quit.
Try not to concern yourself with
when your time will come,
rather keep growing, learning,
and preparing for a great future.
Never stop believing in yourself
and maintain hope, because
miracles happen every single day.

Affirm...

I am patient and expect great things to come.
I visualize my dreams.
I stay determined and positive.

March 1

It will be ok

"Let every moment be what it's going to be.
What's meant to be will come your way.
What's not will fall away.
Relax, don't worry."
Mandy Hale

Remember...

The truth is that you will not always be ok
and that times will be tough.
The good news is that everything will be ok.
When you are feeling weak you need to
stay strong, because everything will be ok.
Just be your own best friend when you are
going through struggle because that is
fa very important relationship.
Keep telling yourself it will be ok, and believe it!

Affirm...

I take comfort in knowing things will be ok.
I know I will be ok.
I support myself and heal.

March 2

Stay in a calm environment

***"You can't calm the storm, so stop trying.
What you can do is calm yourself.
The storm will pass."***
Timber Hawkeye

Today's message...

Sometimes you need to surround yourself
with gentle people for the sake of
having a soft place to fall.
Keep your sweetness and detach yourself
from any bitterness in your world.
A calm environment can help bring
inner strength and confidence.
Surround yourself with people and things
that have a calming effect on you.

Ask yourself...

How can I be gentle and acknowledge that
I am doing the best I can?
What needs to happen in order to be gentle and kind
to myself and others?
How can I choose and direct my thinking
to a peaceful place?

March 3

Be clear on your intentions

"When your intentions are very pure and clear, nature brings support to you."
Sri Sri Ravi Shankar

Today's message...

When you are crystal clear on
your intentions and desires,
you will be amazed what will
show up for you in your life.
When you become clear on your intentions
you will be more inspired to take action.
Do everything with a good heart and positive intentions,
and in return you will never be disappointed.

Ask yourself...

What is the 'why' behind everything I do?
Am I living from habit or living more from intention?
What are my intentions?

March 4

Stay balanced

"Time you enjoy wasting is not wasted time."
Marthe Troly-Curtin

Today's message...

Take time to do things that are fun.
Sometimes we need to step out of
the role of work and responsibility
and into the role of fun and recreation.
It's ok to make time for yourself and have fun.
This will help balance your life and make you feel happier.
Look at all areas of your life and make sure
you are making time to simply waste time.
Don't feel guilty for doing
fun things for yourself.

Ask yourself...

What can I do that is simply fun for me?
What time wasters fill me up with happiness?
What makes me feel energized?

March 5

Keep your head up

***"Don't worry about a thing,
every little thing is gonna be alright."***
Bob Marley

Remember...

Train your mind to see the good
in every single situation and person.
Being positive in a negative situation is a tough
but essential decision you need to make.
Sometimes good things in your life have to
fall apart and crumble in order for new
opportunities to come together.

Affirm...

I focus on good things.
I am staying strong.
I am positive in negative situations.

March 6

Release negative thoughts

"When you let go,
you are creating space
for something better."
Old Saying

Today's message...

Life is a balance between what you
can control and what you cannot.
Let go of the things you cannot control.
Manage what you expect in your life,
limit your need to control,
and peace will come.
Let go of negative thoughts and things in your life,
and replace them with good things and thoughts.

Ask yourself...

How can I let life's events come freely,
and welcome all lessons?
What am I trying to control in my life?
What negative thoughts can I replace
with positive ones?

March 7

Notice abundance all around you

"Don't wait for everything to be perfect before you decide to enjoy your life."
Joyce Meyer

Remember...

Miracles happen every single day,
the problem is you forget to notice them.
Laugh, be grateful, breathe deep,
appreciate, hug, and dream big.
Make wishes and watch them come true!
Refine what it is that you expect in life;
stop expecting and start acting
on your dreams.

Affirm...

I notice all the miracles in my life.
I pay attention and notice abundance all around me.
I properly manage my expectations.

March 8

Respect yourself

"How you treat yourself is how you are inviting the world to treat you."
Unknown

Today's message...

The way that you treat yourself sets the standard
for how you would like the world to treat you.
You have control over how you treat yourself.
Choose to be kind to yourself, eat well,
get plenty of sleep, and exercise.
Love yourself enough to set your boundaries.
Your time, your energy, and your life are all
about your own boundaries that you set.

Affirm...

I treat myself with respect.
I make good choices for myself.
I set healthy boundaries.

March 9

Awaken the power within you

***"Adopting the right attitude
can convert a negative stress
into a positive one."***
Hans Selye

Today's message...

Tap into the power that you have inside you.
Find peace in knowing that everyone
has a super power and special gift.
Make time to focus on what
makes you powerful.
Choose to take notice of
your positive attributes.

Affirm...

I am powerful.
I have special gifts that support me.
I focus on my positive traits.

March 10

Avoid being self-critical or judgmental

"One small positive thought in the morning can change your whole entire day."
Dalai Lama

Today's message...

Try to be your own best friend.
Consider how you talk to yourself in your mind.
Is it nice? Is it encouraging?
Start your day with focusing on your strengths
and what you have to bring to this exciting new day.
Stop or delete negative, self-critical,
or judgmental thoughts about yourself.
Re-write your thinking by building up
your strengths and being nice to yourself.

Affirm...

I am my own best friend.
I delete or cancel negative statements about myself.
I speak loving kind words about myself.

March 11

See the world in a fresh way

"Dear stress, I'm breaking up with you."
Ky-Lee Hanson

Remember...

Life isn't about waiting for opportunity to
come to you but rather you need to get out there
and try new adventures for yourself.
Release the need to fight the old
and welcome the new into your life.

Affirm...

I feel new beginnings coming to me.
I see the world with fresh eyes.
Positive changes are coming my way.

March 12

Reroute your attention

"You can't start the next chapter of your life,
if you keep re-reading the last one."
Unknown

Today's message...

If a bad mood has you in its grip,
remember it is better to have hope
and think positive than to despair.
Choose to chase your dreams instead of
deciding to run from your fears.
Dwell on what is going fantastic,
not on what is going wrong.
Stop dwelling on problems
and focus on solutions or opportunities.

Ask yourself...

How can I talk to myself?
What would hitting the reset button look like?
How can I push through fear and doubt?

March 13

Embrace life with excitement

"Enthusiasm is the sparkle in your eyes,
the swing in your step,
the grip in your hand,
the irresistible surge of will and energy
to execute your ideas."
Henry Ford

Remember...

An enthusiastic heart finds opportunities everywhere.
Stop worrying about what can go wrong,
and get super excited about what can go right.
One of the best ways to get what you want
and find enthusiasm in life is to
be grateful for what you already have.

Affirm...

Today, I am excited about everything.
I am excited about all the good things to come.
I am grateful for my life.

March 14

Take notice of beauty in your life

“***Grace means that all of your mistakes***
now serve a purpose
instead of serving as shame.”
Anne Lamott

Today's message...

Your life is full of beauty, the problem happens
when you don't take notice of this beauty.
Make good choices and remember:
strength comes from overcoming the things
that you once thought you could not do.
Don't give up.
Hard work pays off in the end.

Ask yourself...

How are all my struggles and mistakes
opportunities for learning?
I notice obstacles when I take my eyes off my dreams;
what are my dreams?
How can I challenge myself to be
stronger and more graceful?

March 15

Release old anger, grief, and fear

***"Every time you are tempted
to react in the same old way,
ask if you want to be a prisoner of the past
or a pioneer of the future."***
Deepak Chopra

Remember...

Negative emotions and grudges are
a waste of the person you really are.
Sometimes you need to let go of things.
You deserve the best things in your life;
don't let anger and fear prevent you
from experiencing good things.
Distance yourself from people in your life
that bother you and be open to accept the
positive, strong people that you deserve.

Affirm...

I surround myself with good people.
I let go of toxic negative situations.
I release anger, fear, and grief.

March 16

Connect to your inner power

***"Your mind is a powerful thing.
When you fill it with positive thoughts,
your life will start to change."***
Gautama Buddha

Today's message...

Believe in yourself because you are
more powerful than you may realize;
avoid the nay-sayers and non believers.
You are powerful when you know
that you are capable of anything
and keep focusing on your greatness.
Look inside, that is where your inner strength lies,
not outside of yourself.

Ask yourself...

Am I pulled in the direction of haters?
How can I think of the special people
that matter and really love me?
Life can be challenging;
how can I go out and be powerful?

March 17

Say and look at affirmations regularly

***"Words have the power to both
heal and destroy.
When words are both true and kind,
they can change our world."***
Unknown

Remember...

Keep your eye out for positive events
and occurrences during your day.
Assume the best and see what happens.
Think the best of yourself and others,
and look forward with hope to a great day.
Affirm positive thoughts daily
and keep focusing on what you do want.
Affirmations are simply
a declaration by a person that offers
emotional support, focus, or encouragement.

Affirm...

I believe good things will happen.
I have positive intentions.
I feel gratitude for waking up today.

March 18

Pay attention to your thoughts

***"Whether you think you can
or think you can't,
you're right."***
Henry Ford

Today's message...

Trust your inner hunches and intuition.
They are the best offers of guidance.
Learn from within and many ideas will come to you.
All the answers you need ultimately come from inside you.
Recognize when something is not good for you
and be strong enough to let it go,
you have trustworthy inspirations.

Ask yourself...

When you get confused, you can ask yourself:
"Whom am I listening to?"
What is my own mind telling me?
What song is my heart and mind singing?

March 19

Let go of blame and look for new solutions

"Nobody can go back and start a new beginning, but anyone can start today and make a new ending."
Maria Robinson

Remember…

Let negative experiences in your life motivate you
to be better, stronger, and achieve more.
Let go of feeling hurt or blaming others,
and focus on believing in yourself and all that you are.
The bigger the obstacle,
the greater the victory you will feel when you
persevere and overcome challenge.

Affirm…

I am a warrior.
I choose to focus on strength, courage, and power.
The worst is behind me.

March 20

Use your power to make your life better

"At any given moment
you have the power to say,
this is not how the story
is going to end."
Christine Mason Miller

Today's message...

Take responsibility for your thoughts, feelings and actions,
and you will get your power back immediately.
You are in charge of your life, and you cannot
blame others for anything that is not working in your life.
Your life is a result of your choices.
If you are not happy with your life,
make different choices.
Connect with what you are passionate about.

Ask yourself...

Am I giving other people the power to take my peace?
What decisions do I want to make today?
If I were to be a character in a movie,
what would I have happen,
and how would I describe my character?

March 21

Discover what you love

***"Passion is the reason you journey.
Passion is the fire that lights your way."***
Zehner

Today's message...

People with great passion
can make the impossible happen.
If you can't figure out your purpose,
figure out your passion.
Your passion will lead you right into your purpose.
If life doesn't get better by chance,
it will get better by change.
Go back to your childhood wonder
and make changes that bring about
your passion.

Ask yourself...

What is my passion?
When have I felt passionate?
What brings me happiness and excitement?

March 22

Uplift, motivate, and comfort others

"When life gives you
a hundred reasons to cry,
show life that you have
a thousand reasons to smile!"
Stephenie Meyer

Today's message...

Your life will not get any better simply by chance,
but it will get better with change.
Thinking and being positive is not just about
expecting good things to happen every time,
but about accepting that whatever may happen
is the best for that moment.
Every bad situation and event will have
something positive woven inside it at some point.

Ask yourself...

How do I react to life?
There is a silver lining, or growth opportunity, in
everything; am I willing to see it?
Do I talk about my problems?
Can I try instead to talk about my joys?

March 23

Do what makes you happy

"Do not take life too seriously.
You will never get out of it alive."
Elbert Hubbard

Remember...

Do things that you love, and with passion.
You must have a strong desire to change,
and hope that it is greater than
the desire to stay the same.
The stronger your desire,
the greater your motivation
and achievement will be.

Affirm...

I listen to my heart.
Today, I jump into my life with full effort.
I keep my desire in mind every day.

March 24

Embrace where you feel discontent

"Dissatisfied people change the world."
Old Saying

Today's message...

Being in a state of restlessness or discontent
is a surprisingly good place to be,
since it is the first step towards change.
When you have a strong ambition for things in your life,
dissatisfaction is a symptom you might
experience before taking action.
Accept any feelings of discontent as a message
that you need to fulfill your soul on a deeper level.

Ask yourself...

What feelings of frustration and dissatisfaction
can serve as growth?
If I am not content, how can I fill my life with more?
What can I tell myself and do everyday that will
lift me up and feed my spirit?

March 25

Do what you love

"The meaning of life is to find your gift.
The purpose of life is to give it away."
Pablo Picasso

Remember...

Be open and willing
to take whatever steps
or inspirations call to you.
Passion and purpose
are simply about doing
what you love and staying
dedicated to following your dreams.

Affirm...

I am filled with gifts.
I choose to go with the flow of life.
My purpose and passion are revealing themselves to me.

March 26

Play and laugh

"Every laughing moment you have leaves no room for stress."
Unknown

Today's message...

Friendship is about showing up
with love in times of trouble.
Keep those people in your life that make you
laugh, smile, and feel better.
You deserve to be happy
and have some amazing fun times in your life.
It's nice to have people in your life
that would never judge or criticize you.
People will love you, not for what you look like
or accomplish, but for who you are.

Ask yourself...

Can I think of a true friend in my life?
How can I be crazy, silly, and carefree today?
How do I make people laugh, smile, and feel loved
by being a friend?

March 27

Don't feel isolated

***"The best way to find yourself
is to lose yourself in the service of others."***
Mahatma Gandhi

Today's message...

When you open your heart and help others,
you no longer feel alone.
Associate yourself with people of good qualities
and form your own community.
Surrender yourself to people who
make you feel touched and supported.
Seek kind and loving support from those around you.
Someone out there cares for you.

Ask yourself...

Who can I choose to surround myself with?
Am I the kind of person to others
that I would want to be around?
Do the people around me drain me or do they inspire me?

March 28

Think for yourself

"Take the risk of thinking for yourself. Much more happiness, truth, beauty and wisdom will come to you that way."
Christopher Hitchens

Todays Message...

When you are constantly thinking of,
and worried about,
what others are thinking, saying, or feeling,
you end up trying to people please.
It is important to think about your own
feelings, needs, and perspective first.
There is a peace and strength that comes from
believing in yourself and all that you are.
Know that you are important.

Affirm...

I listen to my own thoughts.
I am worthy.
I think for myself.

March 29

Be vulnerable and try new experiences

"This is about trying new things, getting out of ruts and worry."
Teri Gault

Remember...

Take time to respect other people's opinions
and suggestions, even when you may not agree.
They might have some insight that could help you in life.
Keep working on yourself, and nourish
the relationships around you, so you are ready
when opportunity comes your way.
Allow yourself to be vulnerable;
this is the place of learning, growth, and connection.

Affirm...

I allow myself to be vulnerable.
I am open to receiving.
I grow and learn every day.

March 30

Have courage to step out of the box

"Live your life the way you want.
You'll figure it out."
John Grisham

Today's message...

You are in complete control of yourself.
Growth in your life has to start with your decision
to move forward beyond your current circumstances
and take ownership of your ability to do so.
You don't have to explain your dreams
and aspirations to anyone.
You actually don't need approval from anyone
in order to live your life
and do what makes you happy.

Ask yourself...

How would I describe my character if
I were cast in a movie?
How can I challenge myself today to be better?
How can I stand up for my dreams and myself today?

March 31

Take care of your body

"Treat your body like
the most amazing machine ever designed,
because that's what it is."
Nick Redmond

Today's message...

The physical body is capable of so much,
providing you with life.
Be sure to nourish, respect, and appreciate it.
With a healthy body, your mind and spirit
can live with confidence.
Self-love and self-control is making your
physical, mental, and emotional health
a big priority in your life.
Connect to nature, and you will
find beauty everywhere.

Ask yourself...

How can I keep my food, body, and thoughts clean?
How can I make my environment feel calmer?
When can I make time to take a quiet walk in nature?

April 1

Withdraw your attention

"Let her sleep, for when she wakes she will move mountains."
Napoleon Bonaparte

Today's message...

Rest time is not time wasted,
it is an opportunity to gather strength and wisdom.
Taking time to do nothing often brings everything
back into perspective and helps you regain strength.
Step back and evaluate what is important.
Taking time to self-reflect or examine
is the key to insight and wisdom.

Ask yourself...

How can I listen to myself and take time to rest?
What are the best forms of rest for me?
Sometimes it is ok to take a step back;
what do I need to do to withdraw?

April 2

Monitor your thoughts

***"A year from now,
everything you are stressing about
won't even matter."***
Unknown

Remember...

Your thinking is like an architect for your life.
Nobody can make you negative
unless you decide to become negative.
Your life is a direct result of
the choices you make
on a continual basis.
If you are not happy with your life,
start to make better choices.

Affirm...

I monitor my thoughts.
I am positive and think about what I desire.
My mind is a powerful tool.

April 3

Stay optimistic and expect miracles

"Accept what is,
let go of what was,
have faith in what will be."
Doris Day

Today's message...

Don't give up on what is really important for you,
you will look back one day and be glad you didn't stop.
At times you will face challenges and difficult situations.
Like a caterpillar turns to a beautiful butterfly,
your time to shine will come.
Keep visualizing your success
and take action daily towards your goals.

Ask yourself...

Am I discouraged?
How can I keep growing and preparing for my dreams?
What would it take to visualize the things I want in my life:
see it, feel it, and believe in it?

April 4

Follow your own guidance

"Trust your vibes.
Energy doesn't lie."
Unknown

Todays message...

You know, deep down inside you,
what to do at any given moment.
Your inner voice and gut know best.
Make sure you take time to slow down
and listen to that inner voice.
Often our inner voice is talking to us,
but other people's voices, opinions,
and chatter can get in the way.
Stay strong and connect to that voice
that is YOURS.

Affirm...

I listen to my own voice.
I am wise.
I trust my vibes.

April 5

Have a positive outlook

"A happy person is not a person
in a certain set of circumstances,
but rather a person with
a certain set of attitudes."
Hugh Downs

Today's message...

Objects and circumstances are not the things
that make a person happy.
It is our attitude and ability to see the world
through a lens of appreciation.
Happiness comes from within and not from others.
We have the choice to make ourselves happy
or to make ourselves miserable.
Don't wait for the right moment to start;
shift your perspective to being grateful
and look for good things in your life.

Ask yourself...

What makes me feel like sunshine?
What do I appreciate about my life?
What am I grateful for today?

April 6

Bring on your joy

***"Passion is energy.
Feel the power that
comes from focusing on
what excites you."***
Oprah Winfrey

Remember...

Never underestimate the power of
all the things you have done.
They are preparing you for a great future.
Keep putting your attention and care onto the things
you want to grow in your life.
Follow your true passion and follow
the things in life you naturally enjoy.
Your dream is going to bloom when it is ready.
Enjoy the moment you are in now
and let joy be your magnet.

Affirm...

I am patient and growing everyday.
I put attention onto my dreams.
I nurture my dreams.

April 7

Hold tight

***"Just when the caterpillar thought
the world was ending,
she became a butterfly."***
Barbara Haines Howett

Today's message...

Hold tight.
Just when your world
seems crazy and stressful,
beautiful things will happen.
It's hard to know and find strength
when you are in challenge
or a stormy situation,
but one step at a time,
one breath at at time,
you will get through this.

Affirm...

I choose peace.
I can handle what life throws me.
I am safe.

April 8

Have faith in yourself and your abilities

"Many people think they want things, but they don't really have the strength, the discipline. They are scared. I believe that you get what you want if you want it badly enough."
Sophia Loren

Today's message...

You are able to achieve anything you want.
You have to be willing to invest the necessary energy, time, and effort in order to be successful.
Follow your dreams and have faith in your abilities to accomplish great things.
When you move into self-doubt, tap back into having faith in your abilities.
Look for evidence of your success!
Keep going.

Ask yourself...

Am I trying my hardest?
What else can I do?
How can I strengthen my abilities?

April 9

Maintain inner peace

"You cannot find peace by avoiding life."
Virginia Woolf

Today's message...

Try not to be in a hurry.
Do everything quietly and in a calm spirit.
Even when the world seems upsetting,
try not to lose your inner peace.
Even if your whole world seems upset,
remember somewhere inside you
there is a strength that will
get you through everything.

Affirm...

I choose peace.
I value inner peace.
I am strong inside.

April 10

Trust everything falls into place

"Storms don't last forever."
Unknown

Today's message...

There is a sense of peace in knowing
that everything seems to fall into place.
Just like every time you have been faced with
a challenge you got through it in the end,
you can trust everything will work out for you.
Take time to relax, even amongst stress and challenge.
You are safe, and will be safe.

Affirm...

I am safe.
The challenge will pass.
I trust everything will be ok.

April 11

You are enough

***"If you correct your mind,
the rest of your life
will fall into place."***
Lao Tzu

Today's message...

You have enough strength inside you
to face any adversity.
You are enough.
It doesn't have to make sense right now.
Life is full of ups and downs.
Let your brain relax.
You don't need to stress.
Find a place of peace within.
Don't let the behaviour of others
destroy your inner peace.
Listen to your heart
and quiet your mind.

Affirm...

I am enough.
I listen to my heart.
I quiet my mind.

April 12

Remember lack only exists in the mind;
think abundance

"Worry never robs tomorrow of its sorrow,
it only saps today of its joy."
Leo Buscaglia

Remember...

If you expect the best you will be the best.
Learn to use the power of your mind
and positive thinking to change
your life for the better.
Focusing on lack or deprivation
creates a pattern of lack
and negative predictability.
Instead, occupy your mind with abundance
and anticipate good things.

Affirm...

I expect good things to come.
I notice the positives in my life.
I focus on abundance.

April 13

Expect exciting opportunities

"The best wave of your life is still out there."
Joel F. Crystal

Today's message...

Like surfing, if you don't like the wave you just rode,
get back out there and try another one.
Exciting new opportunities are always around the corner.
Observe ideas and thoughts that enter your mind.
Pay attention to new beginnings,
new ideas, and new energy,
as they can be exciting.

Ask yourself...

Stand or sit quietly and ask yourself:
what great things can happen today?
What new ideas and choices can I entertain?
How can I better listen to my inner voice?

April 14

Turn possibilities into realities

***"Nothing is impossible,
the word itself says 'I'm possible'!"***
Audrey Hepburn

Remember...

Be sure to look for possibilities instead of perfection.
There are opportunities everywhere
and if you don't see them you have to
create them for yourself.
It is better to keep all your options open
than to close your eyes and your thinking.
Just remember, when nothing is entirely sure for you,
anything is possible.

Affirm...

I see unlimited possibilities.
I have options to choose from.
I make changes in my life.

April 15

Enjoy the simple things

"Delight in the little things."
Rudyard Kipling

Today's message...

Take delight in the simplest things in your life.
Find the things and people that
bring you great enjoyment and pleasure.
No matter how serious life gets,
you still need that time to be completely silly.
The best times in life are the ones that
are random and unplanned.
Enjoy the simple things in your life
that bring you joy!

Ask yourself...

How can I be spontaneous?
Today is my day to make things happen: what will I do?
What would my inner child say to my adult self?

April 16

Enjoy music

***"Music is a piece of art
that goes in the ears
and straight to the heart."***
Blackmore

Today's message...

Music can be a powerful tool to shift
your emotions and feelings.
Boost your mood with the power of music.
Learn to let go of things and lift
your emotions listening to music.
Mindfulness is paying attention on purpose,
in the present moment.
Music is a wonderful tool that completely
absorbs us and removes us from worry.

Ask yourself...

What music brings mindfulness and focus in the moment?
What is my favourite music?
Can I observe how music makes me feel,
and how it brings mindfulness?

April 17

Step outside

"Those who don't believe in magic will never find it."
Roald Dahl

Today's message...

Playtime is a form of research and it's amazing what you can discover. Fill your life with playfulness, and you will rediscover the magical world around you. Joy eases your life burdens and renews your sense of optimism as it makes you more open to new exciting possibilities. Sometimes a change of perspective is all it takes to see things in a positive light.

Ask yourself...

What can I do to add more play, laughter, and joy into my life?
Can I take a deep breath?
Where can I go for a walk today?

April 18

Shine your bright light

"Don't let someone dim your light simply because it's shining in their eyes."
Jessica Ainscough

Today's message...

Don't be afraid to be who you are
and shine your bright light.
You make the world a brighter place
just by being you.
Think about when you have been
full of life and sparkle.
What makes you shine bright?

Affirm...

I am enough.
I am full of sparkle and light.
Today, I shine my bright light.

April 19

Your prayers have been answered

***"Pray, not because you need something,
but because you have so much
to be thankful for."***
Henri Nouwen

Today's message...

Value and appreciate all the people, things,
and experiences around you on a daily basis.
Life goes by fast; take time to appreciate
and love the moments.
Give thanks for all the opportunities in your life.
Even your struggles can lead to happiness.
Choose to concentrate on
the abundance in your life.

Ask yourself...

Can I make a list, or simply acknowledge,
all the things I appreciate?
What is going well for me?
What do I love in my life?

April 20

Go with the flow

"Life is a journey with problems to solve, lessons to learn, but most of all, experiences to enjoy."
Ritu Ghatourey

Today's message...

Wanderlust isn't about running away from everything.
It is about taking time to experience the outside world, to discover and experience you.
Look forward to new opportunities, and when they come along you have to grab them.
If opportunities don't come along, go find them.

Ask yourself...

What fears do I have?
What fears might be holding me back from opportunities and adventure?
What would I do if I were not scared?

April 21

Have some fun

"My philosophy is:
If you can't have fun,
there's no sense in doing it."
Paul Walker

Remember...

Today's purpose is to have some fun.
Time flies when you're having fun.
It is your choice how you spend your time.
Take time today to enjoy something.
Try something new if you can't
think of a way to have fun.

Ask yourself...

What does fun mean to me?
What brings me joy?
When was the last time I had fun? What was I doing?

April 22

Rest for now

"I just need a break from everything for a little while."
Unknown

Remember...

Sometimes the easiest and best way
to solve a problem is to stop, step away,
and stop participating in the problem.
Know when to step away from
the busyness of life and gain perspective.
Withdraw your attention from
the world around you and never neglect
an opportunity for improvement.

Affirm...

I need rest.
Today, I will do absolutely nothing.
I step back today and self-examine.

April 23

Notice repetition

"Synchronicity is the universe saying you are getting warmer."
Michelle Risi

Today's message...

Pay attention to meaningful coincidences in your life.
Notice meaningful connections and messages
that happen all around you.
Serendipity is the fortunate discovery,
seemingly by chance,
of something or someone that leads to
other wonderful things happening in your life.
Pay attention to repetition or coincidences!

Ask yourself...

Can I see any patterns and messages?
What am I ready for?
Can I think of times of coincidences?

April 24

Fill yourself up today

"You can't pour from and empty cup.
Take care of yourself first."
Expression

Today's message...

Discover all the things that make you feel
full of life, love, and energy.
These are the things you want to do often.
Conversely, notice the things that
deplete or drain you,
and try to avoid these things.

Today's affirmation...

I choose to do things that fill me up today.
I avoid the people and do less of the things that drain me.
I take care of myself.

April 25

Don't fret

"Creativity is intelligence having fun."
Albert Einstein

Today's message...

Creative thinking inspires new ideas, and ideas inspire change. An essential part of being creative is not being afraid to fail. Rearrange what you know. Find out what you may not have thought of already: this is creativity.

Ask yourself...

What can I do to be creative today?
Can I think of some creative opportunities for my life?
What options can I create?

Remember...

Imagination is the beginning of creation. Creativity is like the incentive for improvement. Have fun exploring opportunities. Remember, worrying will not stop negative things from happening, but it will stop you from enjoying the good things in your life.

April 26

Smile today

"Smiling does not only make you feel more happy and positive, it also increases self-confidence."
Paul Eckman

Today's message...

Use your smile to change the world.
Peace begins with a smile.
Be happy with what you have in your life and catch yourself smiling.

Ask yourself...

What makes me smile?
How can I smile more often?
What moments do I savour?

April 27

Look for happiness inside

"If you are searching for the one person that will change your life, take a look in the mirror."
Unknown

Remember...

Happiness is an inside job.
No person, amount of money, or possession will make you happy. It is your own thinking that determines your own happiness.
There are things you can do to make yourself happier, like practicing kindness, expressing gratitude, doing what you love and enjoy, and surrounding yourself with a great community of friends and family.

Affirm...

I am the only person that can make me happy.
I am in charge of my own life.
If I want change, I can make it.

April 28

Heal and bounce back

"Adversity is the first path to truth."
Lord Byron

Ask yourself...

Do I have any wounds that need healing?
How can I heal at my own pace?
Life needs me, how can I heal, grow, and focus forward?

Remember...

We cannot change the challenges and life experiences we have gone through, but we can learn and focus forward on the next exciting opportunity.
Healing doesn't mean that damage and hurt never existed, it simply means that the challenge is no longer going to take control of your life.

Affirm...

Whatever it takes, I can make it through.
I am healing.
I take action to heal myself.

April 29

Enjoy your life

"There are two things in life
that motivate you:
the fear of pain and the desire for pleasure."
Anthony Robbins

Today's message...

Take the time to enjoy the simple things and find
happiness in the common things in your life.
In the moment where you are, try to be fully present.
Take time to relax.
Try not to take life so seriously that
you start to forget the whole point is
to enjoy it and have fun.

Ask yourself...

What's my guilty pleasure?
How can I remind myself that life is supposed to be fun?
How can I have fun, be crazy, and be silly today?

April 30

Balance

"A mind open to alternative perceptions is a mind aligned with love."
Unknown

Today's message...

Keep your mind open to many opportunities.
Be prepared to look at many options
and from different perspectives.
When you open your mind
your world will open up to you.
Sometimes we feel stuck because
our thinking is stuck.
Balance your life by looking at new perspectives.
A sense of peace comes when
you can see many possibilities.

Ask yourself...

What else can I consider?
How would it look if I looked at this differently?
What am I missing here?

May 1

Stand tall and confident

"Keep your head up.
Keep your heart strong."
Ben Howard

Ask yourself...

How can I tap into the things that make me special?
Who can I be kind towards today?
When have I felt confident and proud?

Remember...

Be humble in your confidence
yet courageous in your character.
You just have to be yourself
and go full with confidence.
Believe that you are enough
and trust in your capabilities.

Affirm...

I am worthy.
I stand tall.
I am sweet and caring to others.

May 2

Notice your progress

"Good things happen when you set your priorities straight."
Scott Cann

Today's message...

You are stronger than you think.
Look at all the things you have already accomplished and gotten through successfully.
You are great, and never doubt yourself.

Ask yourself...

What am I most proud of?
What challenges have I overcome in the past?
What allows me to believe in myself?

Remember...

Whenever you find yourself doubting how far you can go, just remember how far you have already come. Remember everything you have faced,
all the challenges and battles you have won,
and all the fears you have overcome.

May 3

You matter

***"It doesn't matter what others are doing.
It matters what YOU are doing."***
Unknown

Today's Message...

Don't worry about what others think.
Also, try not to compare yourself to what others
are doing. You will feel more at peace if you
just focus on yourself and stay positive.
Just keep moving forward and don't concern
yourself with what anybody thinks. Do what
you have to do, for you. Don't let other people
destroy your inner peace and confidence.
Be courageous and do what you're afraid to do.
Refrain from comparing yourself to others,
and focus on you. Don't be scared to give up things in
your life in order to go for what could be amazing.

Affirm...

I do me.
I choose to focus on myself.
I am doing great things.

May 4

Leave everyone better than they were

"We rise by lifting others."
Robert Ingersoll

Today's message...

Positivity is contagious,
and so is negativity.
Choose to spend more time with
people who think positively,
speak positively,
and who support you.
And be the same for others.

Remember...

When you are a person that lifts others up,
you spread happiness and kindness
throughout the world and create a ripple effect.
Remember to nurture and build people up.
Be one who has an understanding heart
and look for the best in people.

May 5

Be nice to yourself

"If you wouldn't say it to a friend, don't say it to yourself."
Jane Travis

Today's Message...

The way that you speak to yourself, about yourself, really matters. Your words have an impact on your strength, confidence, and level of happiness. When you are mad or disappointed in yourself or a situation, before you speak, think about the words you are about to choose. Talk to yourself like you would talk to someone that you love. Your own mental health is very important and negative, mean words can affect you adversely. Repetitive self-talk is a powerful form of communication because it can empower you, or it can tear you down.

Affirm...

I speak kind words to myself.
I filter my mental chatter.
I am kind to myself.

May 6

Choose peace

"Peace comes from within.
Do not seek it without."
Gautama Buddha

Today's message...

It is possible to choose peace over worry.
Today try not to stress over things
you cannot control.
Decide to choose peace,
and be peaceful today!

Remember...

You can choose calm, patience, faith,
and hope in a moment of stress.
Shift your focus to gratitude for instant peace.

Affirm...

I choose peace.
I am calm and faithful.
I choose not to stress over things.

May 7

Be Positive

"We're so busy watching out for what's just ahead of us that we don't take time to enjoy where we are."
Calvin & Hobbes

Remember...

Take time to look around you for great things.
Appreciate the miracle that life brings.
You can find evidence to prove anything.
Look for evidence of positivity in your life.
The more you look,
the more you will find!

Affirm...

Today is going to be a really good day.
I am excited for new possibilities.
Good things come to me.

May 8

Balance

"Balance is not something you find, it's something you create."
Jana Kingsford

Today's message...

If your life feels like something is missing, seek balance.
Make sure you have a nice blend of fun, friends, family, nature, exercise, and rest.

Affirm...

I choose balance in my life.
I give areas of my life attention that need it.
My life is balanced with work and play.

May 9

Relax

"You have enough.
You do enough.
You are enough.
Relax."
Unknown

Remember...

Find some time to relax, play, and laugh.
While seeking and accomplishing your dreams,
don't forget to also enjoy life.
You don't have to wait for everything to be
perfect before you decide to enjoy life a little.
Take time to sit back and relax.
Recharge your strength with down time.

Affirm...

It's time to have some fun.
Today I enjoy the little things in my life.
I am listening to my need to relax.

May 10

Lighten up

"Life is too important to be taken seriously."
Oscar Wilde

Today's message...

To attract positive energy
and positive things into your life,
you need to give off positive energy.
You have the choice to
make things easy, to lighten up.
Never get jealous when
you see someone having fun,
just create your own fantastic fun time.

Ask yourself...

What can I choose to let go of?
What makes me smile and enjoy myself?
If you stop having fun, ask yourself:
why am I doing these things?

May 11

Choose a good life

***"We are not given a good life or a bad life.
We are given a life, and it's up to us
to make it good or bad."***
Gautama Buddha

Today's Message...

Happiness is a choice and not an end result of
getting something or achieving something.
Nothing will make you happy and content
until you choose to be happy and content.
You can change what you focus on and choose
to be in a happier more content state.
With our own peace of mind and thoughts,
we have the control to find inner peach and happiness.
You can experience inner peace the second you decide
you are in control of your thinking and your focus.

Affirm...

I choose happy.
My life is beautiful.
I am content.

May 12

Try new things

"If you never try, you'll never know what you are capable of."
John Barrow

Today's message...

Life brings you new experiences and opportunities.
Be sure to seize every chance you get
to try something new.
You will learn and grow as a result.

Remember...

Life brings good experiences,
so be open to new adventures
and wonderful changes.

Affirm...

I choose to try new things.
I see my life as opportunities to try.
I learn and grow everyday.

May 13

Appreciate your life

***"Never let the things you want
make you forget about
the things you have."***
Old Saying

Today's message...

Take notice and appreciate
all of the good things in your life.
Having an attitude of gratitude
becomes a daily practice.
You can unwrap each day like a precious
gift that you have received.
Express gratitude in all things in your life.

Ask yourself...

Can I take a moment every day to deliberately notice
at least one beautiful thing in my life?
What am I grateful for in my life today?
How can I choose to have a positive mind
and a grateful attitude about my life?

May 14

Take ownership for your life

"Until you take ownership for your life, you will always be chasing happiness."
Sean Stephenson

Remember...

You are in the driver's seat of your life.
You decide what happens to a large degree.
You are responsible for the actions you take.
Take back your power and own the life
that you are creating.
Make some great choices
today and everyday!

Affirm...

I am in charge of how I feel.
Today, I am choosing happiness.
I make my own reality.

May 15

Look for opportunities

***"Trust yourself.
You have survived a lot
and you will survive
whatever is coming."***
Robert Tew

Today's message...

Every day you have a choice:
you can look for obstacles or opportunities.
Life feels much nicer when you
are continuously asking yourself,
what are the opportunities here?

Ask yourself...

What are the opportunities in my life?
What are the challenges?
What great things can I look forward to?

May 16

Don't compare

"Note to self:
Don't measure your progress using someone else's ruler."
Unknown

Today's Message...

It never feels good to compare yourself to others. Comparison can make you struggle and feel insecure. It's a funny thing when we compare ourselves to others, we tend to measure ourselves up against that person. By not comparing, you are choosing peace and allow yourself to focus on your own story. This self-focus allows you to peacefully be the unique you that only you can be!

Affirm...

I am unique and original.
I am on my own path.
I go at my own pace.

May 17

Choose to be happy

"Happiness looks gorgeous on you."
Old Saying

Today's message...

Beautiful things happen when you distance yourself from negativity and be somebody who makes everybody feel good.
Happiness is a choice.
Take notice of what's good in your life, be grateful, and practice being happy.

Ask yourself...

What is awesome in my life?
Where can I put my attention that makes me happy?
What brings me more happiness?

May 18

Be open to life

"As I say YES to life, life says YES to me!"
Louise Hay

Today's message...

You will enjoy life a lot more by
saying "yes" instead of saying "no".
Saying "yes" to happiness means
learning to say "no" to the things and people
that stress you out or bring you down.
Opportunity does not necessarily knock at your door;
it presents itself when you open it.

Ask yourself...

What can I say "yes" to?
What new experience can I try?
What action can I take to dissolve my fears?

May 19

All that you need is within you

"BElieve in YOURself."
Expression

Today's message...

You have within you right now,
everything you need to deal with whatever
the world may throw at you.
Having a low opinion of yourself is not "modesty".
It's self-destructive.
Hold who you are in high regard.

Affirm...

I am strong and hold myself in high regard.
I have all that I need within me to deal with challenge.
I am enough.

May 20

Rest and nourish your body

"You gotta nourish to flourish."
Expression

Remember...

When you recover or discover things that nourish you,
care enough about yourself to keep
making room for these things in your life.
Eating healthy and respecting your body
is the best approach to self-care.
Look really deeply into nature and spend time there,
you will understand and appreciate everything better.

Affirm...

Every day I am nourishing myself.
Nature feels like home to me.
I see beauty all around me.

May 21

Look at all options

"Sometimes it's the smallest decisions that can change your life forever."
Keri Russell

Today's message...

When feeling confused or uncertain,
you can try to look at all possible options.
Zoom out the lens, and try to see things
from a different perspective.

Ask yourself...

What could I explore?
What part of the situation have I not yet considered?
What other angles can I think of?

May 22

Challenge makes you stronger

"What doesn't kill you make you stronger, stand a little taller."
Kelly Clarkson

Today's message...

Stress and challenge are inevitable in life,
but suffering is an option for you.
See your challenges as opportunities to be strong.
No matter how much it hurts now,
someday you will look back and realize
your struggles changed your life for the better.

Remember...

Every struggle in your life has shaped you
into the person that you are today.
Although it is hard at times, you can be
thankful for those challenges as they
make you stronger every day!

May 23

Be spontaneous

"Over-planning kills magic."
Old Saying

Remember...

Take time to remember what childhood
delight brought you happiness;
chances are it will still bring you excitement.
Be spontaneous, sometimes later becomes never.
When you do things with no explanation, but just
with spontaneity, you can be sure
that you are enjoying yourself.
Let certainty and uncertainty feed off each other,
and find your child-like wonder.

Affirm...

I take delight in my life.
Today, I sprinkle my life with a little silliness.
I am spontaneous.

May 24

Give your spirit joy

"Why push through life when you can dance through it."
Christina Szegedi

Today's message...

Rest and self-care are so important
to keep you balanced.
When you take time to replenish your spirit,
it allows you to be stronger,
and serve others in positive ways.
Life isn't always a party,
but while you are living this life,
you might as well dance and enjoy it.

Ask yourself...

How can I take an hour to play?
My life has an expiration date:
how can I live life to its fullest today?
What replenishes my life force?

May 25

Permission to be human

"It's great to be great,
but it's greater to be human."
Will Rogers

Today's message...

Maybe you don't have perfect hair,
flawless skin, or perfect teeth;
that doesn't mean you're not beautiful.
Maybe you didn't handle a situation
as well as you wish you could have;
that doesn't mean you're not a good person.
Give yourself the permission to be human!

Remember...

There his no such thing as a perfect person.
You come to love yourself and others
not by finding the perfect person,
but by seeing yourself and others
as perfectly imperfect.

Affirm...

I am not perfect and that is ok.
I am human.
Never judge, we are all human.

May 26

Pay close attention

***"You have to pay attention,
get yourself ready for anything,
because you really don't know
what is going to happen."***
Mark Adams

Today's message...

When you really pay attention,
it is amazing how much you end up learning.
It's sweet when someone remembers
every little detail about you,
not because you keep reminding him or her,
but because they pay attention.
Listen to your heart
and pay attention to your intuition.

Ask yourself...

What is life teaching me right now?
How can I be more mindful
and present in my interactions?
What would happen if I spoke less and listened more?

May 27

Do something scary

"Courage is being scared to death, but saddling up anyway."
John Wayne

Today's message...

Try something new and slightly scary today. You will be amazed how facing your fears and pushing through it will bring you to new levels in your life. You will feel a sense of accomplishment and achievement.

Remember...

Always do things that are within safety and that will move you forward towards your goals.
Could I ask that guy or girl out?
Book a flight somewhere?
Send an email asking for that favour?
What have you been putting off out of fear?

Ask yourself...

What would scare me slightly, that I could do today?
What small thing would represent a victory over myself?
What have I been putting off that I can try?

May 28

Choose to make yourself strong

***"We either make ourselves miserable
or we make ourselves strong.
The amount of work is the same."***
Carlos Castenada

Today's message...

When things are not going as well
as expected or desired,
choose to take those moments
to make you better and stronger.

Remember...

Choose to build yourself up in times
of challenge or struggle.
In the long run working on making
yourself better will feel better.

Ask yourself...

What can I do to make myself stronger?
What always makes me feel better?
Is there something I can do to build myself up?

May 29

Be strong

"Being strong doesn't mean you don't feel pain. It means you feel it and try to understand it, so you can grow from it."
Karen Salmansohn

Today's Message...

The best way to approach obstacles in your life
is to use them as an opportunity to learn.
See challenge as an opportunity to learn and grow.
Stay strong in your belief in yourself while
seeing challenge from a growth mindset.
See every mistake from the perspective of
making progress and getting better.
This approach to challenge will bring you
a sense of peace and strength.

Affirm...

I am strong.
I am learning and growing.
Life is my classroom.

May 30

Cheer up those around you

"Try to be a rainbow in someone's cloud."
Maya Angelou

Today's message...

You can make a difference in someone's life
by being beautiful, kind, lovely,
supportive, and compassionate.

Remember...

You may not know or understand
what someone is dealing with in life,
but you can make a huge impact.
You might be the highlight that changes
the trajectory of a persons' life.

Ask yourself...

Is there someone that needs cheering up?
How can I be kind and helpful to someone?
How can I be more compassionate?

May 31

Connect to what brings you joy

"Change is the essence of life;
be willing to surrender who you are
for what you could become."
Norman Vincent Peale

Today's message...

You become light by doing the things
that spark the light inside you.
The first step to getting where you
want to go is having the courage to
get rid of what you don't want.
If you don't like something in your life, change it.

Ask yourself...

What brings me joy?
What can I do that brings me towards my goals?
What do I want to become?

June 1

Endings and new beginnings

"Be kind to yourself while you adjust."
Unknown

Remember...

There are times in your life when you need to
walk away from things so that you can
move forward to something even better.
Never give up.
Remember: the end of one thing is
the start of something else new and exciting.

Affirm...

I am excited about new beginnings.
I wipe my slate clean.
I start fresh.

June 2

Fill your cup

"What if we recharged ourselves as often as we did our phones?"
Unknown

Today's Message...

There is an expression that the best way to recharge your batteries is to unplug from the world for a while.
Make yourself a priority once in a while
and take time to turn inward.
Do something just with yourself and be ok
with being alone with yourself.
This will help to recharge your batteries
and give you a big dose of self-care.
Take a yoga class, spend time polishing your nails,
take a walk, or read a book.
Take time with yourself to upgrade your energy.

Ask Yourself...

What is the best way I can recharge?
What can I do alone with myself?
Who am I when no one is around?

June 3

Ride the current of life

"Sometimes you gotta just go with the flow."
Old Saying

Remember...

Lose yourself in new surroundings
and enjoy finding yourself.
Travel and explore the world around you.
Never lose an opportunity to see
anything that is beautiful and inspiring.
Take every opportunity to ride the wave of life.

Affirm...

It's time for another adventure.
I grab new opportunities.
My adventure begins now.

June 4

Give yourself attention

Today's message...

The greatest gift you can give yourself is
a little bit of your own attention.
Make time for self-care.
Be good to yourself.

Remember...

The love and attention you always thought
you wanted from someone else,
is the love and attention that
you first need to give yourself.
Take time for spa-like treatments,
eating healthy, yoga,
or anything that makes you feel like
you are caring for yourself
and giving yourself the attention
that you deserve.

Ask yourself...

What would make me feel great?
How do I care for myself?
What can I do to give myself the attention I deserve?

June 5

Keep learning

Ask yourself...

How has a time of failure made me stronger?
What opportunities have helped me learn and grow?
How can I cherish experiences more?

Remember...

Part of life's big adventure is learning
and growing from experiences.
Focus forward, grow from,
and learn in moments you may feel broken.
Life is a collection of precious moments,
the trick is to learn from life,
gain wisdom, and enjoy!!

Affirm...

I value my experiences.
I learn everyday and grow wiser.
Past challenges only made me stronger.

June 6

Think positive thoughts

***"Your mind is a powerful thing.
When you fill it with positive thoughts,
your life will start to change."***
Gautama Buddha

Today's message...

Your attitude determines your direction.
Think positive and talk positive and feel positive.

Remember...

Train your mind to see the positive in every situation.
You are the master of your mind.
Don't think about what might go wrong,
but rather think about what might go right for you.

Affirm...

I see positive things all around me.
I choose to focus on the positive.
I am a positive person.

June 7

See opportunities everywhere

"An enthusiastic heart finds opportunities everywhere."
Paulo Coelho

Today's message...

Opportunity is everywhere.
The key is to make sure you develop the vision to see it.
Learn also how to create opportunities for yourself.

Remember...

Keep building your skills and learn everyday
because opportunities will keep
presenting themselves.

Ask yourself...

How can I be creative?
What is possible for me?
What opportunities can I jump on?

June 8

Trust and relax

"Your calm mind is the ultimate weapon against challenges, so relax."
Bryant McGill

Remember...

Luck is not an accident but rather,
it is a meaningful synchronicity.
Be open to the guidance of coincidence,
and pay attention.
Everything happens for a reason,
when you listen and pay attention you will see
clear direction and guidance.

Affirm...

If it's meant to be it will be.
I pay attention to patterns and messages.
I let the universe be an indicator or compass on my path.

June 9

Be disciplined

***"You're not going to master
the rest of your life in one day.
Just relax. Master the day.
Then just keep doing that everyday."***
Unknown

Remember...

Make note of your behaviour;
be impeccable to yourself and others.
If ever there was a time to shine and follow
your passion, the time is right now.
Maintain your power and intention to
start living the life you always imagined.
You don't have to be perfect to be amazing,
be brave enough to start.

Affirm...

I make today ridiculously amazing.
I am impeccable and take action.
I am certain and disciplined.

June 10

Heal yourself

"It's ok to not be ok."
Unknown

Today's Message...

You are not weak for needing time to sort through everything. It's ok to feel deflated and down at times. These emotions are happening to keep you safe. Sometimes you will feel so sad that it physically hurts inside. Sometimes things will not be ok. Talk to yourself with love and kind regard in these times. Just like mothers rock and soothe a crying baby, take time to soothe yourself. Heal your wounds.
Take back your peace and your sparkle.

Ask Yourself...

What makes me feel loved and supported?
What is soothing to me?
What would help me at this time?

Affirm...

I am allowed to cry.
I am allowed to be angry.
I am not allowed to give up.

June 11

Open yourself up to receive

"Abundance is not something we acquire, it's something we tune into."
Wayne Dyer

Today's message...

You are surrounded with an amazing amount of abundance, you simply have to start noticing and appreciating everything. Life offers you many gifts, the problem is when these gifts go unnoticed. Be generous and it will become a part of your growth pattern and prosperous life.

Ask yourself...

How can I be grateful when I find myself in positive situations?
What will allow me to blossom?
How can I be generous with my time, energy, and love?

June 12

You create your own happiness

"Stay calm and do what makes you happy."
Old Saying

Today's message...

You are in charge of your own happiness.
It is not your job to make others happy,
nor will anyone else be able to make you happy.
Nothing will make you happy
until you choose to be happy.

Ask yourself...

What contributes to my happiness?
What can I be grateful for in my life?
When I was happy last, what was the thinking I had
that made me feel happy?

June 13

Be curious

"Open your hands, if you want to be held."
Rumi

Today's message...

Successful people have to take big risks
knowing that they might not succeed.
Take the steps you need to take
and imagine all that is possible.
Your future is created by all the little things you do today.
Lead yourself to new opportunities.
Remain curious and all kinds of interesting new things
will present themselves to you.

Ask yourself...

Imagine no limitations and then decide:
what do I want for myself?
Can I image what I would do, if I could do anything?
How can I be curious today?

June 14

Self-reflection

"Time spent in self-reflection
is never wasted,
it is an intimate date
with yourself."
Paul TP Wong

Today's message...

Take a moment to check in and see
what is going on for you right now.
Take inventory of how your life is going.
What needs your attention and
some adjusting at this time?

Ask yourself...

What gave me the most joy today?
What has caused me the most inner conflict and stress?
What am I grateful for?

June 15

Find music that lifts your spirit

"Music is to the soul
what words are to the mind."
Johnny Depp

Remember...

Music is a piece of art that can be felt in the heart.
Turn the music up and let your heart sing.
Music has shown to be powerful because it has
the capacity to reorganize our brain function.
Lift your emotions by selecting music
that boosts your mood.
Music is a form of
mindfulness and presence.

Affirm...

I enjoy music today.
Music uplifts and supports me.
I boost my mood with great music.

June 16

Transform

"What you seek is seeking you."
Rumi

Remember...

Life is a blend of both positive and negative,
your reaction to situations literally has
the power to change the situation itself.
Invent the life you desire.
You sometimes have to adjust your thinking
and living to transform your life,
like Thomas Manson's quote,
"You can't control the wind, but you can adjust your sails."

Affirm...

I change negatives into positives.
I am inventive with my life.
I am grateful for all the good things
and not so great things in my life.

June 17

Think happy thoughts

"Happiness does not depend on what you have or who you are. It solely relies on what you think."
Gautama Buddha

Today's message...

Think happy thoughts.
When you think you're not happy with your life, know that your happiness depends upon what you are thinking.

Remember...

Most people think happiness is about gaining something, but it's not.
It's all about working on your thinking and being grateful for everything you have and are.

Ask yourself...

How can I express kindness?
What am I grateful for today?
What do I appreciate about my life?

June 18

Filter your world

***"See the world through
rose coloured glasses."***
Old Saying

Today's message...

The world you see is created by what you focus on.
It is never too late to adjust how you see the world.
Your experiences and past have formed a filter
through which you see the world.
Sometimes we have to adjust the story
we might be telling ourselves.

Ask yourself...

How do I choose to interpret the world?
What lens am I seeing the world through?
Can I change my lens?

Affirm...

I see the beauty that life has to offer.
I see the beauty within myself.
I choose to see the world beautiful.

June 19

Good friends

"You become like the five people you spend the most time with. Choose carefully."
Jim Rohn

Today's message...

Surround yourself with people that reflect who you want to be. Choose friends that force you to be and do better.

Remember...

Your friends should motivate and inspire you.
People around you should be supportive.
Quality is more important than quantity.

Ask yourself...

Are my friends bringing out my best?
Who are my quality friends?
Who brings out my best?

June 20

Make good choices

"May your choices reflect your hopes,
not your fears."
Nelson Mandela

Ask yourself...

What is important to me?
How can I follow my own heart, live my own passion, and find deep meaning?
How do I know I'm making good choices?

Remember...

We are all confronted with countless choices each day. The key is to honour your priorities and be brave enough to let go of what isn't working in your life. You deserve happiness and deep down inside, you know what you need to do.

Affirm...

Today I am a priority.
I choose to follow my heart and make good choices.
I let go of what isn't serving me.

June 21

Have some fun

"Be bright like glitter
and bubbly like champagne."
Old Saying

Remember...

Never put off the fun you could have today until tomorrow.
Be playful and give yourself a break
that might be much needed.
Embrace uncertainty; some of the most fun
and unexpected beautiful moments
are found in uncertainty.
Having fun allows you to shine bright!

Affirm...

I am going to lighten up.
Let's have fun today.
I enjoy myself.

June 22

Set boundaries

***"Life is a balance of
holding on and letting go."***
Rumi

Remember...

Boundaries are a part of self-care.
They are healthy and necessary.
Give thanks and take nothing for granted.
Balance your life with fun,
laughter, and positive people.
Be sure to compromise,
but never give up your values
and what is important to you.
Make sure your compassion
includes yourself.

Affirm...

Today, I set boundaries.
I choose to balance give and take.
I am compassionate with myself.

June 23

React to life positively

"Life is 10% what happens to us and 90% how we react to it."
Denis P. Kimbro

Today's message...

Be mindful of how you react
to things in your life.
A positive mind looks for
ways it can be done;
a negative mind looks for
ways it cannot be done.

Remember...

You can deal with everything
life throws at you.
Choose to react as positively
as you can to challenge.

June 24

Mind power

***"Your mind is everything.
What you think, you become."***
Gautama Buddha

Remember...

Your mind is very powerful.
Whether you think you can or think you can't, either way you are right.
You can use the power of your mind to see life through a growth mindset.
Life feels calmer and more comfortable when you approach life with a mindset of opportunities.

Affirm...

I change my mind, I change my life.
My mind is powerful.
I am careful with my thoughts.

June 25

Life is a classroom

"Every day may not be good...
but there is something good in every day."
Alice Morse Earle

Today's message...

Life is like a classroom where
we live and learn everyday.
Be sure to remain curious and learn
from all of your experiences.

Ask yourself...

What can I learn?
How can the course of the day highlight
any perspective or behavioural shifts
that need to be made?
What can I learn from this?

June 26

Take time for self-care

"Your heart is the most powerful organ. It breaks, heals, and becomes stronger again."
Old Saying

Today's message...

Keep focusing forward and never look back.
Look back only for the lessons that
you can learn from your experiences.
Everything has the ability to heal.
Open your heart to receive healing
and let your heart smile.
Release any burden and take
action to heal yourself.

Ask yourself...

Can I take time to heal at my own pace?
Do I have any wounds that need healing?
Life needs me, how can I heal, grow, and focus forward?

June 27

Love yourself

"Stay away from people who make you feel like you are hard to love."
Unknown

Today's Message...

Life is meant to be a beautiful, fun,
and magical experience.
Spend your time with the people
who make you laugh and feel loved.
Don't let other people bring you down.
Stop letting people control your happiness.
Be yourself and remember who you are.
You are lovable.
Let any haters or negative people
become your motivators.
You have control over whether or not you let
someone's negative behaviours affect you.

Ask Yourself...

Who is trying to bring me down?
What is occupying my mind right now?
How can I keep calm and carry on positively?

June 28

Focus on abundance and prosperity

"Work harder than you think you did yesterday."
Alex Elle

Today's message...

If you dream big you need to work hard,
stay focused, and surround yourself with
good people and situations.
Your effort is required in order to achieve great things.
You can live your life at a new level,
you are the only thing holding you back.
Devote yourself to new learning
and a new level of mastery.
Work with all your heart.

Ask yourself...

How can I start working harder than I did yesterday?
What does the best version of me look like?
Can I think big and act big, but most importantly,
do what I love?

June 29

Remain calm

"With self-discipline, most anything is possible."
Theodore Roosevelt

Today's message...

Take charge of how you want to run your day.
Be very disciplined with yourself
and do what needs to be done.
Being calm, and exercising self-control
is not the absence of freedom,
but rather it will become
the source of freedom.

Ask yourself...

How can I exercise self-control?
What would make me more disciplined?
How can I take action today towards my goals?

June 30

Let go and take action

"Don't dwell on what went wrong.
Instead focus on what to do next.
Spend your energies on moving forward."
Denis Waitley

Today's message...

Keep your head high
no matter what happens.
You'll be all right.
If the moment hurts,
do not fall victim or dwell;
learn, let go, and focus forward.
Don't look in any direction but ahead.

Ask yourself...

What do I need to let go?
What actions, thoughts, or situations do I need to let go?
What can I move forward on?

July 1

Let your spirit glow

"Shine with all you have. When someone tries to blow you out, just take their oxygen and burn brighter."
Katelyn S. Irons

Ask yourself...

What people and situations dim my light?
When do I feel I have lost my sparkle?
Can I transform my state and look for my sparkle?

Remember...

Every time you take away negative energy
from your life your spirit glows brighter.
Allow your inner spirit to glow brightly and outwards;
your brightness will help people who are in darkness.
We all have demons and sometimes darkness;
make changes to uplift your emotional state.

Affirm...

I shine bright.
My spirit glows.
I can change my state, and
I choose to radiate brightness.

July 2

Be self-determined

***"I am not what happened to me,
I am what I choose to become."***
Carl Jung

Today's message...

The only person you are destined to become
is the person that you decide to be.
Even if no one believes in you
and what you desire for yourself,
keep going.

Affirm...

I will be happy with who I am today.
I will keep fighting for who I desire to be tomorrow.
I am determined.

Andrea is available for:

Coaching, Writing, Workshops,
Webinars, Book Clubs and School visits!

Reach out at:

www.andreaseydel.com
andrea.livelifehappy@gmail.com

416-456-7555

ABOUT THE AUTHOR
Andrea Seydel

"The opportunity to be a rainbow in someone else's cloud - makes my heart sing."

Every day may not be good but there is something good in everyday. It's my job (passion) to spread the science of well-being, and offer a toolkit of support and resources to help others move towards their mental, physical and life goals. When I connect with people I strive to energize and inspire them to live a fun, happy, and meaningful life. Every single ounce of my formal education has played a role in my holistic approach to coaching, training, and writing. It is a great pleasure to train, educate, and coach clients around the subject of positive psychology, self-development, and well-being. I have a degree in psychology from York University and have taken post-graduate studies in nutrition and applied positive psychology. Through my early work as a nutritionist in weight loss and life coaching, I've discovered a widespread need for psychological support around self-efficacy, effective thinking strategies, and communication. With a passion for NLP and the power of our language, I was trained in Non-Violent Communication.

I also care very much for the mental health of our teens and young adults. I love spending time teaching resiliency skills to teens and young adults as a suicide intervention, as well as anxiety and depression First Aid.

Remember, "Every dark cloud has a silver lining."
Life is NOT perfect, but I believe we can
find that silver lining!

Hugs, Andrea

IF YOU LOVED THIS BOOK, YOU'LL LOVE THIS FREE GIFT & THE LIVE LIFE HAPPY COMMUNITY EVEN MORE!

TEEN EMPOWERMENT WORKSHEETS
Go to: andreaseydel.com/worksheets

JOIN MY ONLINE COMMUNITY

www.andreaseydel.com

@livelifehappy_teens

@livelifehappy_as

Facebook: Livelifehappycommunity

Podcast: Live Life Happy with Andrea Seydel

YouTube: Live Life Happy with Andrea Seydel

DAILY EMPOWERMENTS SERIES

AVAILABLE IN ALL BOOKSTORES & ONLINE

Discounts available:
Great gift idea for schools, support programs, or employment assistant Program etc. Discounts on quantity purchases are available.
Please email andrea.livelifehappy@gmail.com.

Random act of kindness suggestion: How would you feel if this book arrived in the mail from amazon just for you randomly? May I suggest ordering and sending this book to someone that could use extra support!
You never know the difference you can make!

It's a great day to have a great day!!

December 31

Enjoy knowing you're in loving care

***"Having someone help you
doesn't mean you failed,
it just means you are not alone."***
Johnny Iuzzini

Today's message...

Sometimes accepting help is tougher than
offering help to someone.
Life can be easier if you accept support from people.
You can't do everything alone,
you were born to be real, not perfect.
Take time to retreat and focus on
how you can build your energy up
for new exciting things.
Through thick and thin you are supported.

Ask yourself...

Do I know when I need to ask for help?
What can I do to rest and recharge?
Who surrounds me and supports me, no matter what?

December 30

Be compassionate

***"Namaste: My soul honours your soul.
I honour the place in you where love, light,
truth, beauty, and peace reside, because it is
also within me. In sharing these things
we are united, we are the same, we are one."***
Yoga Adage

Today's message...

Consider that we are all connected as humans.
We all have struggle, challenge, and heartache.
When we understand others perspective
we are better able to be compassionate
and understanding of others.
True peace and love come from
this place of understanding.

Affirm...

I put good out into the world.
I am empathetic.
I love myself and others.

December 29

Trust your desire for change

"Your desire to change must be greater than your desire to stay the same."
Unknown

Today's message...

Give birth to something new in your life.
It takes courage to show up for your life
and try something new.
There is a spark inside everyone,
you just have to fire it up and let that spark shine.
Uncertainty and mystery are a part of life.

Ask yourself...

Is it time to start something new
and have a new beginning?
What would I do if I had a chance for a fresh start?
What part of my life do I desire to change?

December 28

Know you are protected

"May angels fly with you,
wherever you roam
and guide you back safely
to family and home."
Mary Jac

Today's message...

Become what you wish and get rid of what you don't need.
Mentally know that all the things you think about
will be supported if they are meant to be.
What you put your mental attention on,
you will attract that thought into your life.
Find ways to feel at peace and have faith.

Remember...

The law of attraction states that
you attract the energy that you give off.
Positive thoughts generate good, positive feelings
and that attracts positive life experiences.
Life with inner peace is harmonious and flowing.
When you are ok with how things are in your life,
your thinking sends out a positive energy
that attracts more good things into your life.

December 27

Journal your inner nudges

"Journaling is like whispering to one's self and listening at the same time."
Mina Murray

Today's message...

Journaling allows you to calm your mind
and connect to your inner self.
That is where your soul lives and the music is playing.
When you are worried, it's probably that
you are trying to figure out everything on your own.
When you write down your thoughts and inner nudges,
you allow for healing, harmony, and clarity.

Ask yourself...

Can I look deep inside my heart, by writing in my journal?
If everything lies within, how can I take time to look inside?
Can I look for answers in the pages of my journal?

December 26

You're guided in beautiful ways

"If you're brave enough to say goodbye, life will reward you with a new hello."
Paulo Coelho

Today's message...

Being self-aware is not absence of mistakes,
but rather the ability to learn, grow, and correct mistakes.
You are guided in beautiful ways in life,
but awareness allows you to get outside
of your mind and observe your guidance.
Detours in your life may lead to discovering
places you never knew you would love.
Embrace guidance and potential.

Remember...

Pay attention, as eventually all things fall into place.
Let go and don't doubt that you are
supported through challenging times.
Good things will come soon
and look for the beauty in
the unexpected moments.

December 25

Choose your battles

"Be selective with your battles. Sometimes peace is better than being right."
Unknown

Today's message...

Choose gentleness today. Speak in a soft voice. Move in a smooth slow manner. Choose smooth motion activities like you yoga. Listen to soft music. Let yourself be silent and turn inward. Try not to engage in or participate in any battles. There are times when it is healthier to choose peace and turn inward.

Ask yourself...

What would bring me peace to day?
How do I find calm amongst the world?
What makes my heart calm?

December 24

Be gentle with yourself and others

"A kind gesture can reach a wound that only compassion can heal."
Dr. Steve Maraboli

Today's message...

When you share pieces of your heart with others,
your heart actually grows bigger and more beautiful.
If you know how it feels to be alone,
take time to be there for people.
Accept yourself and others unconditionally.
Honour who you are today,
and not who you wish to be in the future.

Ask yourself...

How can a little consideration and thought
make other people's lives better?
How can I care for others and feel loved?
What ways can I accept and love myself, flaws and all?

December 23

Create new routine

"Make it a great day or not, the choice is yours."
Unknown

Remember...

Try to go somewhere you have never been before.
Unless you try to do something beyond
your comfort zone you have already experienced,
your life will not change.
Life gets boring if you stay within the limits
of what you already know.
Try something new each and everyday.

Affirm...

I take a deep breath and break free.
I try new things.
Today, I explore new ways.

December 22

Ease up and rest

"Do not confuse your bad days as a sign of weakness. Those are actually the days you are fighting the hardest."
Old Saying

Today's message...

In life, as we go forward, there are times of mental and physical exhaustion. Fatigue is different than being tired. When you are tired, sleep can remedy. But if fatigue is still there when you wake up, and it stays all day, it's time to take a much-needed break. Even in darkness, it is possible to create new light for yourself.

Ask yourself...

How can I be nice to myself?
What would a break to restore my life look like?
Be careful how you are talking to yourself: how can I ease up on myself?

December 21

Clear clutter and feel lighter

"Solitude is the place of purification."
Martin Buber

Today's message...

Purify your life by keeping your space,
your body, and your mind clean.
Make a decision to clear clutter in your space.
Clutter represents indecisions and things that
distract you from fully living your life.
Release what is no longer
serving you in a good way;
you'll feel lighter, and your space
will function much better than before.

Ask yourself...

What people, things, or activities do I need to let go of?
How can I be selective of when, where, and how
I invest my time and energy?
When have I made space for me to be me?

December 20

Practice energy boosting activities

"Where attention goes energy flows."
James Redfield

Remember...

It is essential to realize that over time as you get upset,
it drains you emotionally and energetically.
Now is the time for better habits, positive thinking,
eating clean, and loving yourself.
The higher your energy,
the more efficient your body is,
the better you feel.

Affirm...

I am full of positive energy.
I spread positive life force.
I practice energy boosting activities.

December 19

Remove chaos and simplify

"Simplicity is the ultimate sophistication."
Leonardo Da Vinci

Today's message...

Never overlook the power of simplicity.
Simplicity is simple and elegant.
Clutter is a physical manifestation of uncertainty,
that can cripple your ability to grow
and reflects your mental state.
Sometimes you have to let go,
so that there is room for better things
to come into your life.

Ask yourself...

What are the most important things in my life?
How can I clear clutter and make space in my life?
What is unproductive and distracting in my life
that I can throw out or get rid of?

December 18

Let go of what is not working

"Healing comes when we choose to walk away from darkness and move towards a brighter light"
Dieter F. Uchtodor

Today's message...

Give yourself time to heal.
Healing does not mean that damage
never existed or didn't take place,
it means that it no longer
takes a hold of your life.
Walk away from darkness
and focus on what's really good.
Your mistakes are not challenges in your life
but they become the problem when
you allow them to define you.

Ask yourself...

What wounds do I have that need healing?
How am I doing well?
What can I focus on in order to move forward?

December 17

Be kind to yourself

"Never say anything about yourself you wouldn't want to come true."
Brian Tracy

Today's message...

Talk to yourself like you would to someone you love.
The words we say to ourselves have power
and they affect us tremendously.
Be aware of any negative or mean things
that you might say to yourself.

Ask yourself...

Am I hard on myself?
What are better thought options for me?
How can I be kinder to myself today?

December 16

Visualize, imagine, and explore

"Dream as if you have forever.
Live as if you have only today."
James Dean

Remember...

Daydreaming helps you believe
things can get even better.
Let the universe hear your dreams
and get excited to see the magic
that unfolds in your life.
Make sure you visualize
what you really want and desire.
Welcome each day with
the joy and wonder of a child.

Affirm...

Today, I awaken my inner child.
I step away from life and day dream.
I visualize, dream, and imagine.

December 15

Stand tall and proud

"Be like a pineapple:
stand tall,
wear a crown,
and be sweet on the inside"
Expression

Today's message...

Own your own truth and be confident.
Remain humble and kind on the inside.
You can be confident and love yourself
while being sweet and caring
all at the same time.

Affirm...

I am proud of me.
I am confident.
I love myself.

December 14

Be understanding of others

***"Peace cannot be kept by force;
it can only be achieved by understanding."***
Albert Einstein

Remember...

You never know what other people are dealing with,
be patient and understanding.
Hold back any judgment or critical thoughts
towards others and try to understand instead.
Don't hold onto your anger or bitterness
as it is like drinking something poisonous.
Choose instead to approach hurt with a loving heart.

Affirm...

I am compassionate.
I forgive others for peace.
I respect others' point of view.

December 13

Remember how lovable you are

***"Good friends are like stars,
you don't always see them
but you know they're always there."***
Old Saying

Today's message...

Be sure to surround yourself with
people that make you happy;
the people that make you laugh,
who help you when you need support.
Choose to be around those friends
that genuinely care about you.
There is an expression that you become
like the five people you spend the most time with.
Since we are influenced by the people around us,
your circle of friends should encourage
your growth and happiness.

Ask yourself...

Can I think of a true friend in my life?
How can I be a good friend today?
How do I make people laugh, smile,
and feel love by being a friend?

December 12

Practice appreciating

***"Gratitude dissolves negativity.
Decide that no matter what comes your way,
you'll find a grateful heart."***
Unknown

Today's message...

Appreciation is a wonderful tool to use to help you
see and notice what is really positive in your life.
Gratitude gives you the ability to see
love, joy, and abundance.
Appreciation allows you to see everything that
is already right in front of you that is amazing.
Take time to be thankful and express this
gratefulness to those in your life.
When you are in the moment you are in,
being grateful for what you already have,
you will experience happiness and balance.

Affirm...

I can find joy in my life when I look for it.
I have an extraordinary life.
I value all the good things around me today.

December 11

Believe the best is yet to come

"Forget all the reasons why it won't work and believe the one reason why it will."
Jon Chandonnet

Today's message...

Don't be pushed by your problems or any obstacles.
Be led by your dreams instead.
Always remember the future belongs to the people
who see possibilities before they are obvious.
Look for possibilities and have faith in what will be.

Remember...

You are braver than you believe,
stronger than you seem,
and smarter than you think.
You were given this life because
you are strong enough to life it well.
Don't be afraid to start over
and have the chance to rebuild
what you desire.

December 10

Make time to relax

"Sometimes you just have to stop, take a deep breath and put things into perspective."
Katrina Mayer

Today's message...

Take time to relax and unplug from your busy world.
A tranquil state brings a feeling of freedom
from agitation and stress.
Make some time for yourself today so you can
relax, reflect, and renew your spirit.
Find the calm in the chaos by stepping out
and pampering yourself.

Ask yourself...

What makes me happy?
What is my best kind of pampering?
How can I choose to be kind to myself?

December 9

Clear your energy

"A negative mind will never give you a positive life."
Ziad K. Abdelnour

Remember...

Everything is energy and made up of energy.
What you think about is what you become
and attract into your life.
People like to be around those who
give off positive energy.
Never underestimate the power of thought,
choose your thoughts wisely.
Clear toxic thinking
and be open and positive.

Affirm...

Today, I vibrate good energy into others.
I fill my life with positive energy.
I think good clean thoughts.

December 8

Take back your power

"The way to have power is to take it."
Boss Tweed

Today's message...

Express your own strengths.
Don't let others define who you are
and what your strengths and weaknesses might be.
You are capable of anything,
stand in your power
and connect with your strengths.
You are unique and not one person can be like you,
that is your power.

Ask yourself...

What would make me feel more powerful?
What are my strengths?
What are my super powers?

December 7

Positive breakthrough

"Breakthroughs happen when limiting thoughts and behaviors are challenged."
Fabienne Fredrickson

Today's message...

Success comes when your continued persistence
breaks through resistance.
If you are prepared, you will be confident,
and you will be ready to face opportunity.
Until you spread your wings,
you will have no idea of just how high
you might be able to fly.

Remember...

Ask for what you want and be prepared to get it.
Once you decide to try something,
see it through to fruition.
Your beliefs are like a magnet
to create your own reality.
Drop or let go of limiting thoughts.
Remember the only thing that is
limiting you in life is in fact your beliefs.
Your life is full of unlimited possibilities.

December 6

Use feelings as guidance

"Feelings are like waves,
we can't stop them from coming,
but we can choose which ones to surf."
Jonatan Martensson

Today's message...

Let your smile and happiness change the world,
don't let the world change your smile.
You decide what you put your attention onto.
Honour your feelings and inklings.
Identify and claim feelings that
positively serve you.

Remember...

Each day focus your attention on what you want.
Make up your mind to be happier today.
No matter what, let go of negative emotions or situations.
You have the power to change
your mood, thoughts, and emotions.

December 5

Detach from situations

"When you finally let go of the past,
something better comes along."
Sonia Ricotti

Today's message...

Sometime it will hurt to let go,
but it may hurt more to hold on to the past.
Have you heard the expression
'you can't read the next chapter of your life
if you keep re-reading the last chapter?'
When you let go you make space
for something better.

Ask yourself...

What do I have to do for me right now?
How do I let go of what I can't change?
Are there elements in my life I can't change?

December 4

No need to rush

***"Don't cry over the past,
it's gone.
Don't stress about the future,
it hasn't arrived.
Live in the present
and make it beautiful."***
Unknown

Remember...

Don't rush into things, practice patience
and keep a good attitude.
While you are working hard
things will fall into place.
You are the missing piece
of someone's life puzzle,
you never know where
you are going to fit,
but you will.

Affirm...

I am patient.
My life is unfolding as it should.
I pay attention and have faith in my life.

December 3

Gain clarity

"You get what you focus on,
so focus on what you want."
Unknown

Today's message...

The more clear you are on what you desire
and how you want to show up in this world,
the easier it is to balance your life.
Often times we focus on what we don't want
and dwell on all the things we don't like.
Think about what it is you desire most for yourself
and get very clear on that vision.

Ask yourself...

What is the part of my life that is not yet clear?
What do I want?
What would be the best outcome?

December 2

Find your own awesome

"Be yourself, everyone else is taken."
Oscar Wilde

Today's message...

Don't be afraid of your own personal power.
Don't let anyone dull the sparkle that lies inside you.
You have the power to create your own magnificence.
If there is something you don't like about your life, change it.
Have faith in your abilities with confidence.

Ask yourself...

How can I be my own kind of awesome?
What will make me remember who I was, before the opinion of others decided who I should be?
What makes me special, unique, and powerful?

December 1

Stop self-criticism

"The difference between shame and guilt is the difference between 'I am bad' and 'I did something bad'."
Brene Brown

Today's message...

Try not to be so hard on yourself because you are living and learning everyday.
Sometimes it is ok to not always be ok, don't be so hard on yourself.
Learn how to love yourself for everything you are.
Don't be afraid to love yourself and enjoy the person you are, and are becoming.

Ask yourself...

How can I stop myself when I am being self-critical?
How can I be on my own team?
How can I feel beautiful without needing anyone telling me?

November 30

Prioritize

"Live your truth.
Express your love.
Share your enthusiasm.
Take action towards your dreams.
Walk your talk.
Dance and sing to your music.
Embrace your blessings.
Make today worth remembering."
Dr. Steve Maraboli

Today's message...

What needs your top focus and priority today?
You can choose what gets your attention,
and the choice is entirely up to you.
What needs your attention and effort today?

Ask yourself...

Which parts of my day require my total presence?
Who is it important that I come through for?
How can I reduce non-important,
non-urgent junk from my life?

November 29

Trust in hidden benefits

"Pain and suffering are the soil of strength and courage."
Lurlene McDaniel

Today's message...

There is a reward to any pain and it is experience.
It is hard while you are in the pain of suffering
to see the potential gifts and learning,
but strength will be born.
Create some time to have personal space
for your soul to recover, rest, and think.
Suffering is the school where your heart and soul
can learn and become strong.

Affirm...

I am strong.
I learn and grow.
Tough times will end.

November 28

Don't let your thinking hold you back

***"The greatest weapon against stress
is our ability to choose
one thought over another."***
William James

Remember...

The limit of what is possible for you
only exists in your head.
Your beliefs become your thoughts,
and your thoughts become your actions and habits.
Until you believe you have options,
you'll continue to feel stuck.
Try not to look at life in terms of black or white
because there are many versions of grey
hiding in between.
Think with options in mind
and challenge limiting thinking,
as you will move from excuses to progress.

Affirm...

I have many options.
I challenge any limiting thoughts.
I have an open mind.

November 27

You are getting there

***"Ask yourself if what you're doing today
is getting you closer to
where you want to be tomorrow."***
Unknown

Today's message...

Each day is a wonderful learning opportunity.
We will not always be a huge success
and some days will be really challenging,
but you are continually learning and growing.
Don't get discouraged when things don't seem like
they are working, you are getting there.

Affirm...

I may not be there yet, but I am getting better everyday.
I am continually learning and growing.
I see my life as a classroom.

November 26

Don't hesitate

"Hustle isn't just working on the things you like. It means doing the things you don't enjoy so you can do the things you love."
Unknown

Remember...

Taking action is a wonderful way to remove any doubt from your mind. Believe in yourself and really go for it. If something excites you and makes you a bit nervous as well, just go for it. Don't be afraid to try something new, you never know how much it could change your life.

Affirm...

The time is now for me.
Opportunities are knocking.
I forge forward towards my dreams.

November 25

Be determined

***"No goal was ever met
without a little sweat."***
Unknown

Today's message...

There is so much motivation
and grit when you stay true
to what it is you desire
in your life.
Let no one or any obstacle
stand in your way.

Affirm...

I am a strong and determined person.
I am committed to what is important to me.
I continue to strive.

November 24

Direct your energy

"The secret of change is to focus all of your energy not on fighting the old, but on building the new."

Socrates

Today's message...

Since you cannot always control
what goes on outside of you,
try to control what goes on inside of you.
Direct your energy to positive ways of thinking
and you will feel much more at peace.
When you focus on the good things in your life
you will feel confident and safe.

Ask yourself...

How can I be mindful of my self-talk?
What are the internal conversations I am having
with myself? Are they positive or negative?
What in my life makes me feel safe and loved?

November 23

Accept the things I cannot change

**"God grant me the serenity to
accept the things I cannot change,
courage to change the things I can,
and the wisdom to know the difference."**
Serenity Prayer

Todays message...

Inner peace comes from recognizing
that you choose your emotions
and how other people affect you.
When you make the discovery to let go
of the things in your life that you cannot change,
you will be at peace.
Trying to change someone or a situation
that you have no control over is a
recipe for stress and distress.
Choose peace in the moment you are in
by accepting the things in your life
that you cannot change.

Affirm...

I honour the things in my life I cannot change.
I accept the things I cannot change.
I have courage to change the things I can.

November 22

Enjoy nature outdoors

"For one minute, walk outside.
Stand there in silence.
Look up at the sky
and contemplate
how amazing life is."
Unknown

Remember...

Log off and shut down all your technology
for a chance to go outside.
Nature helps you wake up and feel alive.
It feels good to get lost in nature
and be present in the moment
where the real gifts are found.
Albert Einstein said it best:
"Look deep into nature,
and then you will understand
everything better."

Affirm...

Today, I enjoy the great outdoors.
I renew my spirit with nature.
I am part of nature and I am beautiful.

November 21

Be gentle with yourself

***"Be nice to yourself,
it's hard to be happy
when someone is mean
to you all the time."***
Christine Arylo

Today's message...

Try not to be hard on yourself.
Notice when you are being mean to yourself
with negative self-talk.
Recognize that you are a human,
growing, evolving, and learning everyday.

Remember...

Just when the caterpillar thought
the world was over, it became a butterfly.
Be gentle with yourself,
you are doing the best you can.

November 20

Love your life

"Interrupt anxiety with gratitude."
Danielle Laporte

Today's message...

When you notice and love what you have,
you will have everything you need in this moment.
Get so busy loving your life that you don't
have time to worry, fret, or have fear.
Exercise being grateful and appreciate your life.

Remember...

Happiness is a choice, not an end result.
Your happiness will only come from you.
Some days you just have to create your own sunshine.
It is not selfish to take care of yourself
and make your own happiness a priority.

November 19

Take time to check in

"Sometimes when we get overwhelmed, we forget how big our soul is."
Unknown

Ask yourself...

What is most important to me?
What do I think is best for me?
What resonates most for me?

Today's message...

Take time to turn your focus
onto yourself today.
Be sure to listen to your own needs
and what is important to you.

Affirm...

I honour my inner voice.
I trust my intuition.
I listen to my deepest desires today.

November 18

Love yourself first

***"Self-love is not selfish;
you cannot truly love another
until you know how to
love yourself."***
Unknown

Today's message...

How can you expect other people
to love you when you yourself are
finding flaws and being rude to yourself?
Be kind to yourself
and notice how paying attention to
your greatness feels much better.

Remember...

Pay attention to your thinking
and notice when that inner critic takes over.
Hit the pretend delete or cancel button,
and replace that thought with a better one.
Stop negative self-talk.
Talk to yourself like you are
your own best friend.

November 17

Anything is possible

"Calm mind brings inner strength and self-confidence."
Dalai Lama

Remember...

You can be anything you want to be in this life;
look inside and let the real you shine.
It takes great courage to change your life.
You can literally be or do anything,
but you have to believe it is possible.
Sometimes you have to be willing to
let go of the life you may have planned,
so you can have the life that is waiting for you.
What do you want?

Affirm...

I look inward and find my joy.
I choose to do things that light me up.
I have courage to let go of old habits.

November 16

Take time to breathe

***"I will breathe. I will think of solutions.
I will not let my worry control me.
I will not let stress level break me.
I will simply breathe and it will be okay."***
Shayne McClendon

Remember...

A deep inhalation followed by an exhalation
can change your body physiology
from stressed to being relaxed.
Inhale confidence and exhale doubt.
Sometimes all you need is to step outside
and get some fresh air to remind yourself
of who you are and who you want to be.
Enjoy the moments that you are in,
as they don't last forever.

Affirm...

Let me live, let me take a breath.
I love the feeling of fresh air in my lungs.
I stop and take a deep breath.

November 15

Compete with yourself

"If you compete with others
you become bitter.
If you compete with yourself
you become better."
Unknown

Remember...

Remember, a challenge only becomes
an obstacle if you decide that it is.
Challenge yourself every day to do better
and be better than you were yesterday.
Avoid the temptation to compete
or compare with other people.
But blinders on and run your own race.

Affirm...

Everyday I am getting better.
I see others as inspiration.
Today I challenge myself.

November 14

Nobody is perfect

"Today I will live in acceptance rather than expectation."
Louise Hay

Remember...

You don't have to like everything
about yourself to love yourself.
There will be things that bother you about yourself
and things you wish you could change.
But don't dwell on these things,
they will only bring you down.

Affirm...

I love myself, flaws and all.
I choose to focus on my good qualities.
I focus on my strengths and beauty today.

November 13

Have faith in perfect timing

"Everything you need comes to you in perfect time, space, and sequence."
Louise Hay

Today's message...

No matter what is placed in front of you,
it's a part of your path.
It is important to follow, trust,
believe, forgive, and be grateful.
Sometimes it takes the worst pain
to bring about the best change.
Train your mind to see the good
in every situation and challenge.

Remember...

One day everything will make perfect sense.
Have faith that everything will work out for the best.
Perfect timing is the ability to turn limitation
into new, creative possibilities.
It's up to you to find beauty in the ugly days.

November 12

Wire your brain for positivity

"Train your mind to see
the good in everything."
Old Saying

Today's message...

Your strongest muscle that
you can work is your mind.
Train it well to see
the good in every situation.
Positivity is a choice.

Ask yourself...

What if I could see the positive?
What is good in my life?
How can I start noticing the good in my life?

November 11

Be aware of your feelings

"Sad hurts, but it's a healthy feeling. It is a necessary thing to feel."
J.K.Rowling

Today's message...

Tell someone how you feel.
Write in your journal how you are feeling.
Your feelings are trying to
communicate something to you.
Listen to what you are feeling,
as feelings are messengers.

Remember...

You are human, and being human
means you have feelings.
Feelings are a way of communicating.
What are you feelings telling you?

November 10

Be strong

"Strength doesn't come from
what you can do.
It comes from overcoming the things
you once thought you couldn't."
Rikki Rogers

Today's message...

Sometimes you just have to be strong
even when it is the toughest thing that you can do.
Stand up for what you believe in
and what is true for you.
Keep your head up
and face what you need to face.

Remember...

You were made to do amazing things.
Keep your head up and believe in yourself.
True strength is keeping things together
when everyone expects you to fall apart.

November 9

Stop self-criticism

"Be kind to yourself;
you are amazing,
you are good enough,
and you are worthy."
Elizabeth Gaskell

Today's message...

Open your heart.
It's time to work on you for yourself.
Loving yourself means acceptance,
kindness, and genuine self-care.
If you have been criticizing yourself for a long time,
take notice, try approving of yourself,
and see how it makes you feel.
Take action today in order to remove
any doubt that you might have.

Affirm...

I speak kind to myself.
I open my heart to self kindness.
I love myself.

November 8

Use others as inspiration

"Wanting to be someone else is a waste of the person that you are."
Marilyn Monroe

Today's message...

When you catch yourself comparing yourself to others
and wishing you were more like someone else,
stop yourself.
Instead, approach the situation
as an opportunity for inspiration and influence
to make yourself better and more uniquely you.

Remember...

Stay true to who you are, and use others as
a chance to be an inspiration
and opportunity to be creative
to add to the great person that you already are.
Be who you are.

November 7

Be confident in your own skin

"Confidence is not 'They will like me.' Confidence is 'I'll be fine if they don't.'"
Christina Grimme

Today's message...

What you think of yourself
is much more important than
what people think of you.
Have confidence in yourself.
Don't second-guess who you are.
Who you are is beautiful.
It is none of your business
what other people think of you!

Ask yourself...

When did I last feel confident? Why?
What makes me feel confident?
How can I believe in myself more?

November 6

Move in the direction of your dreams

"Set a goal that makes you want to jump out of bed in the morning."
Brian Tracy

Today's message...

You were born to be a winner,
but to be a winner you need to
prepare and expect to win.
Good things come to those who
embrace their heart's desire.
Stop waiting and start doing,
now is the time.
Take full responsibility for your life,
move forward in the direction you desire.

Affirm...

I follow my dreams daily.
I am capable.
I take baby steps everyday.

November 5

Restriction might be in your mind

"Challenge your self-limiting beliefs.
Most of them are not true at all."
Old Saying

Today's message...

Sometimes your biggest bully
and greatest challenge is yourself.
Henry Ford said, "whether you think you can,
or think you can't, you're right."
Don't limit yourself to what you think you can't do;
push further and think about what you can do.
The only limits in your life are the ones
that you create with your own mind.

Ask yourself...

What self-limiting beliefs can I challenge?
How can I take responsibility for everything in my life?
If I feel "stuck" in a situation,
can I re-evaluate my thinking?

November 4

Clear your space

"Clutter is not just physical stuff. It's old ideas, toxic relationships, and bad habits. Clutter is anything that does not support your better self."

Eleanor Brownn

Remember…

Take notice your environment.
Clear your head by clearing your space.
According to Feng Shui, when you
throw out the physical clutter,
you clear your mind, and when you
throw out mental clutter, you clear your soul.
Choose light healthy foods for your body,
and de-clutter even your diet.

Affirm…

I need a clear view and space.
I shift my energy and clear.
I release anything not serving me.

November 3

Step beyond your limitations

"Freedom is being you
without anyone's permission."
Steven Goad

Today's message...

Freedom is when you realize that
you can do absolutely anything.
Accept that you were born to be great.
Express yourself and don't mind
what other people say.
Decide once and for all
that you deserve to have an extraordinary life
and that you are unique.

Ask yourself...

What am I holding back from?
What would I do if I wasn't afraid?
What is a different way to look at this limitation?

November 2

Be patient and caring

"Even after all this time the Sun never says to the Earth 'You owe me.' Look what happens with a love like that. It lights the whole sky."

Hāfiz

Remember...

Unconditional love is a beautiful gift
that you can give to others
and that you can receive.
Be sure not to expect people
to fully understand you,
but do expect them to
accept and love you unconditionally.
Being able to be patient and caring
in your relationships will help bring
relationship harmony.

Ask yourself...

Am I being loving towards others?
Am I being loved?
How can I remain non-judgmental to an imperfect person?

November 1

Follow what is important to you

***"The cost of not following your heart,
is spending the rest of your life
wishing you had."***
Unknown

Today's message...

Trust what you love, and continue to do
the things that are important to you.
Do them often.
By following your passion and by
doing what is important to you,
your path will become clear.
Your life will flow with ease
and feel "right" when you stay true
to what is important to you.

Ask yourself...

What is most important to me?
How can I build my life around what is important to me?
What would I do if I put myself on the top
of my to do list today?

October 31

Be present and notice opportunities

"The most precious gift we can offer others is our presence. When mindfulness embraces those we love, they will bloom like flowers."
Thich Nhat Hanh

Remember...

You cannot possibly plan life every step of the way, you would miss the turns and twists life has to offer. Dream passionately and remain grateful for all the gifts around you. Abundance follows gratitude. The more you appreciate, the more you will be perceptive to the abundance in your life. Be present and mindful with your thoughts and experiences.

Affirm...

I am full of gratitude.
Opportunities are surrounding me.
I notice all the gifts around me.

October 30

Complete tasks

***"The day she let go of the things
that were weighing her down
was the day she began
to shine the brightest."***
Katrina Mayer

Remember...

Organize your life around your passion
and don't put off things until tomorrow,
if you can do them today.
Sometimes procrastination can weigh us down.
The expression, "don't stop when you are tired,
you can stop when you are done",
really emphasizes finishing projects.
Taking charge of your schedule is a part of
taking charge of your life.

Affirm...

I run my day and my schedule.
I am motivated and organized.
I take control of clutter and organize my life.

October 29

Make positive changes and heal

"Your life does not get better by chance,
it gets better by change."
Jim Rohn

Today's message...

Life has a funny way of working out,
just when you start to believe it isn't going as planned.
Everything in your life is a reflection of
the choices that you have made.
If you desire a different result,
you can make different choices.

Remember...

The decisions you make are choices
and they reflect your life in every way.
Sometimes you need to be alone
and be brave in order to reflect back on life.
Take time to look at where you have been
and where you want to go.
Transform old patterns of your mind
and let go of thoughts that don't serve you well.

October 28

Allow positive energy to flow

"Everything around us is made up of energy. To attract positive things in your life, start by giving off positive energy."
Ralph Waldo Emerson

Today's message...

You are the most important person in your life,
so be sure to take time everyday
to restore your vitality and energy.
People can inspire you, or they can drain you.
Focus on what excites you and fires your passion.
Allow positive energy to flow through you.
Walk away from negative energy
and don't even give it attention.

Ask yourself...

Energy flows where my attention has the tendency to go:
what am I focusing on?
How can I be mindful of my thoughts?
How can I take care of myself,
and remove any energy drains?

October 27

Seek harmony and peace

"Family is a life jacket in the stormy sea of life."
J. K. Rowling

Remember...

Family isn't always about
the people in your life
that are blood relations;
it's about the people in your life
who want you in it.
These people support, love,
and choose to align with you.
Find peace, strength, and harmony
in knowing you have
people who know you well
and support you unconditionally.

Affirm...

I appreciate my family and my roots.
I surround myself with people who care unconditionally.
I love those around me.

October 26

Let goals keep you on track

"Don't be pushed by your problems. Be led by your dreams."
Ralph Waldo Emmerson

Today's message...

Stay focused on your goals and picture the end results so you have a clear image of what you can achieve. Put your attention on the things that you would like to accomplish. Don't compare yourself to others, stay focused on your own journey and ignore the "noise".

Ask yourself...

What goals have I set for myself?
What is my top priority?
If I am in control of my thoughts, what can I do to gain focus?

October 25

Explore new ways

"Sometimes, you find yourself in the middle of nowhere, and sometimes, in the middle of nowhere, you find yourself."
Stacy Westfall

Today's message...

Be brave enough to explore, grow, and break free.
If you want to fly, you need to break away
from the things that weigh you down.
If you explore, you will discover yourself
and collect new exciting moments.
Explore new possibilities for yourself
and watch your world open up to you.

Ask yourself...

Is my routine mundane?
Am I standing on the line between giving up
and seeing how much I can take?
What can I do differently?

October 24

Honour your beauty

"Be your own kind of beautiful."
Marilyn Monroe

Today's message...

You are one of a kind.
There is no chance of a replica.
Beauty is deeper than just your face and your body;
it is the light in your heart.
Seek grace and beauty in all the people
around you and you will find it will also
become who you are.
You are beautiful and not one person, image,
or comment has the right to make you feel
like you are not beautiful.

Ask yourself...

How can I concentrate on finding my inner beauty,
my inner love, and my inner joy?
What can I develop on my own?
Can I acknowledge the things in my life that are beautiful?

October 23

Connect to what inspires you

"Never give up on something that you can't go a day without thinking about."
Winston Churchill

Today's message...

Discipline is doing what needs to be done, even on those days you don't feel like doing it.
Never give up on your dreams.
Let go of any fears that prevent you from achieving your life desires.
Reactivate your dreams on a regular basis and connect to your source of energy.

Ask yourself...

What makes me excited?
What do I do when no one is watching?
What brings me energy?

October 22

Focus on what is great

***"Keep your face always
towards the sunshine
and the shadows
will fall behind you."***
Walt Whitman

Remember...

Pain is an inevitable part of life,
but the suffering that comes from holding onto
the pain too long is optional.
Shift your perception to focus on
good things in your life.
Be strong because things will get better.
Positive thinking and focus will
keep your face towards the sunshine
and you will rarely look back at your shadow.

Affirm...

Today, I heal and feel well.
I focus on what is going great.
I let go of what isn't working.

October 21

Trust and be open

"Old ways won't open new doors."
Old Saying

Remember...

When you are open and willing
to receive support and love,
the universe will open doors and hands to you.
Have faith in your journey and in the fact that
everything had to happen exactly as it has
in order to guide you in the right direction.
See the light in your heart,
and all the people around you.
Believe in yourself and others.

Ask yourself...

Am I using up my energy with worry and fear?
Can I think of any people that can help me?
How can I have more faith?

October 20

Observe without judgment

***"When you judge another,
you do not define them,
you define yourself."***
Wayne Dyer

Remember...

Let the power of love and peace
overpower any struggle or judgment.
Instead of letting people pull you
into drama or tension,
pull them into your peace instead.
Let your joy, love, and beauty
rise to the surface.

Ask yourself...

Can I fill my mind with non-judgmental thinking
and fill my life with peace?
How can I see and listen with love?
Real beauty lies beneath the surface of my skin:
what makes me beautiful?

October 19

Simplify your life

"The hardest thing in the world to do is to simplify your life; it's so easy to make it complex."
Yvon Chouinard

Remember...

Simplicity is uncomplicated and easy.
Life can be complicated if we make it that way.
Life becomes lighter and brighter
when you focus on what truly matters.
Rid yourself of clutter, both mentally, and physically,
to keep peace and calm in your life.

Affirm...

I simplify and de-clutter my life.
I remove mental chaos.
I feel calm and focus on what matters.

October 18

Take time for inner reflection

***"Do not look for a sanctuary
in anyone except yourself."***
Wolfgang Mozart

Today's message...

Go within everyday and you will find inner strength
as you listen to your own guidance, voice, and intuition.
Returning to a place of solitude is stillness.
When you go within and connect with your true self,
you realize true strength.
Listen to your inner voice and follow it,
because it is actually who you really are.

Ask yourself...

How can I shut out the world and go within?
How can I become a little wiser ever day
simply by observing?
My inner voice is who I really am:
what is it saying?

October 17

Be on your own team

"***Work on being in love with the person in the mirror who has been through so much but is still standing.***"
Unknown

Today's message...

Be confident in who you are.
You are unique, beautiful,
and the only person
on this earth like you.
Notice your talents, your skills,
and natural abilities.

Ask yourself...

How can I cheer myself on?
What would my own personal cheerleader say to me?
What are my own character strengths or super powers?

October 16

Fill your life with positive energy

"Positive energy attracts positive energy."
Micheal J. Tamura

Today's message...

The only way to make your world better
is to make an effort to change yourself.
You put off an energy field that
affects the world around you,
work on keeping your energy
positive and balanced.
Clear away toxic, negative thoughts
from your thinking.

Ask yourself...

Do I need to adjust the relationships
around me, or myself?
Consider what and how you are thinking:
Can I grow thoughts in my mind that will produce
a beautiful bouquet of flowers?

October 15

Give yourself some space

"Peace is the result of retraining your mind to process life as it is, rather than as you think it should be."
Dr. Wayne W. Dyer

Remember...

Next time you are exhausted, take a step back.
You need to give yourself more love and affection.
Be kind to yourself, you are amazing and good enough.
Ease up and be nice to yourself, life can
be hard and challenging at times.
See things as they are,
and be ok with that.

Affirm...

I ease up on myself.
I am patient and trust that breathing space is good.
I am kind to myself.

October 14

Self-acceptance and self-love

"Awakening self-acceptance
makes space for inner peace."
Old Saying

Ask yourself...

How can I be more kind to myself?
What makes me who I am?
When was the last time I was proud of myself? Why?

Today's message...

Today is a great day to fully accept the person that you have become. We don't always give ourself credit for the lives we have touched or for the people we are becoming. Remember that you are a special gift to this world. Loving and accepting yourself brings a wonderful sense of peace and tranquility.

Affirm...

I approve of myself.
I love myself.
I am unique and beautiful.

October 13

New day

***"Each morning, we are born again.
What we do today is what matters most."***
Gautama Buddha

Today's message...

It's a fresh new day, with new energy and opportunities.
Start your day with a fresh thankful mind.
Rise and shine bright throughout your day.
See today as a wonderful opportunity
to start fresh and positively.
See today with renewed spirit.

Affirm...

It's a great day to have a great day.
I am excited about what today will bring.
It's a fresh start today.

October 12

Take a break

"It is ok to take a break."
Unknown

Remember...

Balance, peace, and joy
are all states that allow you to
gain positive perspective on your life.
Take time to be still and relax.
It is not selfish to love and care for yourself.
Find ways to pamper yourself
and make your happiness a priority.

Affirm...

I am having a little me time.
I am balanced and pampered.
I am peaceful and take time to relax.

October 11

Purify your space and thoughts

"Never organize what you can discard."
Unknown

Remember...

De-clutter your life and feel the sense of purification.
Have nothing in your house that you do not find
useful or believe it is beautiful.
Think of all the things that are weighing you down.
Not just things, but also habits, thoughts, or people.
Get rid of all that clutter.
The more you can let go,
the lighter you will feel.

Affirm...

I let go of clutter.
I cleanse my space and de-clutter.
I purify my thoughts.

October 10

Add and subtract from your life

"Less stuff.
More Space.
Less stress.
More life."
Unknown

Today's message...

Access what needs to be added into your life that you might be lacking, and decide what needs to be taken out of your life that may be getting in the way.

Ask yourself...

What's missing in my life?
How can I see the whole world new each day?
How can I have fun today?
How can I bring more joy into my life?
What do I want more of in my life?
What do I want less of in my life?

October 9

Expect good things to happen

"Just because the past didn't turn out like you wanted it to, doesn't mean your future can't be better than you ever imagined."
Ziad K. Abdelnour

Todays message...

People will change in your life, things will go wrong, bad situations will happen, but life goes on. You have to move on and trust that everything happens for a reason. Sometimes things are going to hurt and upset you and sometimes it is going to be hard. But in the end it's for the best and you will be ok. When bad things happen, don't let the situation define you or destroy you. Let it strengthen you.

Affirm...

Tough challenges strengthen me.
I am strong.
I expect great things.

October 8

Give your cares and worries away

"Love is the bridge between you and everything."
Rumi

Today's message...

Trust that you will be ok.
Take a deep breath,
and take care of yourself.
When you feel overwhelmed and you're
taking everything in your own hands,
remember: the world is here to help.
Everyone, at certain times in their lives, needs to
take advice and receive help from others.

Affirm...

I have faith things will work out for me.
I give my worries and cares away.
I accept support and help from others.

October 7

Focus on you

"Working on myself,
by myself,
for myself."
Expression

Today's message...

You create your own opportunities.
You are entirely up to you.

Ask yourself...

What do I want most for myself right now?
What could I do to make myself better today?
What opportunities could I create for me?

October 6

Don't worry about what people think

"What you think of me
is none of my business."
Terry Cole-Whittaker

Today's message....

Not caring what people think
is the best choice you will ever make.
Don't worry about others' opinions,
just focus on yourself and stay positive.
Some people will always have something to say,
so don't let others bother you.

Ask yourself...

Does it really matter what others think about me?
How can I put my life, dreams, and goals above
the importance of what others think of me?

October 5

Baby steps

"Do something today that your future self will thank you for."
Unknown

Today's message...

We have a tendency to forget that baby steps
will keep you moving forward.
Slow progress is better than no progress at all.
Focus on what you can do,
not on what you can't do right now.
Keep moving forward
and as long as you're moving
you will get closer to your dreams.

Affirm...

I am getting closer to my dreams.
I take steps every day.
I believe in myself.

October 4

Focus forward

**"Don't stress the could haves.
If it should have, it would have."**
Old Saying

Remember...

It is not always about fixing
what is broken or not working,
but rather, it is about starting over,
and creating something new and even better.
Making big life changes or transitions is sometimes scary,
but you won't live with any regrets.

Affirm...

I am moving on.
I focus forward and make room for new.
I let go emotionally and feel lighter.

October 3

Breathe deep

"Sometimes we just have to let things go."
Unknown

Today's message...

Take a deep breath.
Release the stress, learn, and let go.
Overthinking is just a painful reminder
that you care too much,
even when you shouldn't.

Affirm...

I choose to release all hurt and drama.
I embrace peace and gratitude.
I let go of stress.

October 2

Be patient

"Patience is passion tamed."
Lyman Abbott

Today's message...

Be patient and trust that everything is
falling into place for you.
Don't feel urgency or rushed,
when the timing is right it will happen.
Everything falls into place.
You need all the pieces of a puzzle
to see the entire picture.
You may be missing some
pieces of your life puzzle.

Ask yourself...

How can I trust that I will be put in the right place,
at the right time?
If I just planted new seeds in my garden,
how long would it take them to grow?
How can I exercise being patient while my life
buds and grows beautifully?

October 1

Follow your path

"Let people live their truth without it threatening yours."
Brooke Hampton

Today's message...

Keep moving towards your dreams.
Passion is what draws you in,
excites you, and propels you.
Keep going towards where
life is calling you to go.

Ask yourself...

What is life calling of me?
Which is worse: failing or never trying?
What do I want most in life?

September 30

Look for joy

***"You have dealt with so much,
and done the best that you can,
take a moment now to appreciate
how strong you are."***
Karen Salmansohn

Today's message...

There are things to be joyful about everywhere around you, you simply need to notice and pay attention to the good things in your life. If you pay attention the things that bring you joy, you will notice more things that bring you joy. Be careful what you put your attention on and choose where you focus your attention.

Ask yourself...

What makes me joyful?
What would make me happy?
When have I been joyful in the past?

September 29

Face your fear and forge forward

"The future depends on what you do today."
Mahatma Gandhi

Today's message...

Taking action may not always bring results right away, but it is the most effective way to go about creating a life you desire.
Vision and goals with no action will only be a dream.
You have to take action to create a future you desire.
Wake up everyday stronger and more determined than the day before.

Ask yourself...

What do I have to do to get the life I desire?
What brings me excitement?
What would I do if I wasn't afraid?

September 28

Be open to possibilities

"Sometimes the questions are complicated and the answers are simple."
Dr. Seuss

Remember...

Be open to change and new opportunities.
All it takes is one new insight or idea
to give you that spark of
excitement, inspiration and action.
Sometimes you just have to let go,
don't over think, and simply see what happens.
Tomorrow is a fresh start with no mistakes in it,
what feels like the end might be a new beginning.

Affirm...

I am open to new beginnings.
I try new things.
Each day is a gift with new possibilities.

September 27

Take time to daydream

"Imagination is more important than knowledge. Imagination can take you anywhere."
Albert Einstein

Today's message...

Everything starts as somebody's daydream. Use your daydreams to help you imagine what your future may look like, play with options, and explore possibilities. Spend time every day visualizing another detail of your perfect future. Keep your child-like wonder and enthusiasm alive.

Ask yourself...

What fun things can I imagine and visualize?
How clear am I when visualizing my dreams?
When can I step away from life and connect to my child-like wonder?

September 26

Look for gifts

"Honor the space between no longer and not yet."
Nancy Levin

Remember…

Pain and suffering are inevitable at some point in your life,
but love and healing step forward to help.
Remember the kindest hearts melt the most pain.
Surround yourself with kind, caring people.
Sometimes you just need to take time alone
and that's ok.

Affirm…

I am strong and the pain will pass.
Every one of my challenges is a hidden gift.
I am getting mentally stronger.

September 25

Check in

**"Love yourself and be hopeful,
because you have so much ahead of you."**
Austin Rhodes

Today's message...

Take time to listen to yourself and check in with how you are feeling or thinking. Pay attention to your thoughts and feelings.

Ask yourself...

How am I feeling right now?
How can I enjoy my life today?
What is it I need today?

Affirm...

I check in with myself today.
I am aware of my needs.
I listen to my inner voice.

September 24

Find strength from challenge

**"Courage is not about having
the strength to go on; it is going on
when you don't have the strength."**
Teddy Roosevelt

Today's message...

When everything seems dark and challenging,
know that you will come out the other side stronger.
It's ok to feel weak or broken at times.
It's in these moments that
your strength can grow.

Remember...

It is during the darkest moments
or the rainiest days that we must
focus hard to see the light.
Stay positive and trust
things will work out beautifully.
Tomorrow is another day
filled with opportunities and possibilities.

September 23

Choose harmony

"I believe in creating healthy habits that nourish, not restrictions that punish."
Unknown

Remember...

It is a beautiful thing to stay silent
when someone expects you to act out in anger.
Inner peace will begin when you choose
not to allow others to control your emotions.
Have a criteria for your thoughts
and the people around you;
the criteria can be simply asking yourself,
"have they brought me inner peace?"

Affirm...

Today, I create healthy habits.
I breathe deeply and forgive.
I trust in harmony and find inner peace.

September 22

Set goals for the future

***"Don't stress.
Do your best.
Forget the rest."***
Unknown

Remember…

Victory belongs to the people that
believe in it the most.
You can be angry at life
for not giving you what you want,
or you can feel blessed for
being given all that you need.
Set aside the pain from the past,
enjoy the blessings of the present,
and look forward to the future.
Set your goals, but then focus on
the present moment full of gifts.

Affirm…

Today, I focus on my blessings.
I am peaceful and appreciative.
I trust good things will keep happening for me.

September 21

If you don't like something, change it

"Today I have the power to change my story." Unknown

Today's message...

Incredible changes can happen in your life when you decide that you can take control of what you want. You have the power to make things very different. Embrace the things that you do not have control over and change the things you can.

Affirm...

I have the power to create change in my life.
I can change my story if I want to.
I have the power to change.

September 20

Stop trying so hard

"You are perfect exactly as you are; there is no need to change anything except the thoughts that you aren't good enough."
Unknown

Today's message...

Stop trying so hard for people who don't care.
Stop trying to fit in, you are perfect how you are.
Avoid thinking so hard about everything.
Stop over analyzing.
Just go.
Just be, and if it feels right,
just go with the flow.

Affirm...

I go with the flow.
I am perfect being me.
I enjoy the flow of life.

September 19

Dissolve stress

***"Never stress over things you can't change.
The past is in the past,
and it's not worth your attention."***
Old Saying

Today's message...

Don't stress over what you can't control.
Just let it be and focus on being happy.
Remember nothing is permanent,
so don't stress too much,
because no matter how bad
the situation gets,
it will change.

Affirm...

I breathe in confidence, and exhale stress.
I take each day one at a time.
No point in me stressing.

September 18

Notice what is good

***"It's so easy to look around
and notice what's wrong.
It takes practice to see what's right."***
Melody Beattie

Today's message...

When you embrace the power of gratitude, you will notice that your ability to see beauty all around you increases. Be grateful and appreciative of all those people and things in your life.

Remember...

What you pay attention to in your life is what makes up your experience. You can choose to pay attention to all the good things that show up.

September 17

Have faith in your abilities

"Believe in yourself
and you will be unstoppable."
Old Saying

Today's message...

Stop worrying how it's going to happen
and start believing that it will.
Stand strong, believe in yourself,
and chase your dreams.

Remember...

Your wings already exist.
All you need to do is FLY!
Know that there is something great inside you,
and that you are greater than any obstacle.

September 16

Surround yourself with good people

"You cannot expect to live a positive life if you hang out with negative people."
Joel Osteen

Today's message...

Be picky whom you keep around you.
Associate yourself with good people of good quality.
Choose people who have dreams, desires, and ambition.
If you surround yourself with positive people
who build you up, the sky is the limit for you.

Affirm...

I am kind.
I am lovable.
I am compassionate and caring.

September 15

Be comfortable being you

"Let you smile change the world, but don't let the world change your smile."
Unknown

Remember...

You have the freedom to be yourself
and don't let anyone or anything
stand in your way of fully expressing yourself.
If you are different than the people around you,
don't be ashamed or worried about it,
be who you are, because who you are
is unique and special.
Life becomes much easier
when you accept and embrace
the person you have become.

Affirm...

I am comfortable in my own skin.
I embrace the person that I am.
I am growing and learning while being me.

September 14

Just breathe

"Just breathe.
You'll never live this moment again."
Old Saying

Today's message...

Just breathe: inhale positive life giving oxygen,
and exhale tension and stress.
Sometimes all you need is a breath of fresh air
to oxygenate your body and mind.
Feel like you are inhaling love and exhaling hate.
All you need might be just some time to breathe.
Take time to enjoy every moment of your life.

Ask yourself...

Can I close my eyes, relax my body,
and take a deep inhalation - hold my breath for as long
as I can - then slowly exhale?
Could I set a time to remind myself
to take deep breathing breaks?

September 13

Be kind and sweet

"Be kind whenever possible.
It is always possible."
Dalai Lama

Today's message...

Exercise compassion and curiosity
instead of judging and opinions.
You never know what someone might be dealing with,
so exercise kindness and compassion.

Ask yourself...

How can I be caring today?
What makes me a kind person?
How can I be more understanding?

Remember...

Be that person the makes the world a nicer place
because of who you are inside.
Tap into that place of love and care.
Remember to be kind.

September 12

Choose good friends

"True friends say good things behind your back and bad things to your face."
Unknown

Remember...

Sometimes you have to let people go.
Everyone who is in your life is meant to be there,
but not all of them need to stay there until the end.
Without judgment, listen to your intuition
and don't waste energy on people who
don't appreciate who you are.

Affirm...

I surround myself with people that raise me up.
I choose compassion.
I enjoy the positive people in my life.

September 11

Choose how you feel

"Nobody can hurt me without my permission."
Mahatma Gandhi

Today's message...

You have a choice in every moment.
You can choose to get upset or judge,
or you can choose to learn and be compassionate.
You decide how things affect you with your thinking.
If you want to feel better,
choose a better feeling thought.

Ask yourself...

How can I learn from this situation?
What can I think that will make me feel better?
What is a better feeling thought?

September 10

Accept yourself exactly as you are

"Self-worth is not determined by others."
Old Saying

Today's message...

Try your best to accept yourself unconditionally,
no matter what flaws or traits you think might exist.
You are beautiful, bright, and amazing
in your own special way.
The problem arises when you don't believe this is true.
Put a halt on those things that conspire to
hold you back or bring you down.

Affirm...

I determine my self-worth.
I speak kind to myself.
I keep my self-talk positive.

September 9

Trust your inner voice

"TOLD YOU SO.
Sincerely, your intuition."
Old Saying

Today's message...

The more you trust your intuition,
the more empowered you become,
as this provides insight and support.
This voice is who you really are and deserves attention.
Your inner voice or intuitions are your hunches that
usually help direct you and keep you safe.

Ask yourself...

What is my inner voice telling me?
Do I remember who I was before the world told me
to be different?
What does my intuition say before my thinking interrupts?

September 8

Get outside

"Adventure is just outside your window."
Sadaf Zarrar

Today's message...

Nature has the amazing ability to
restore your senses and renew your spirit.
Wilderness may not be considered a luxury to
many people, but it is certainly necessary for
the renewal of the human spirit.
Take a walk in the woods and notice
you will come out of the trees much taller.
You are part of the natural world - beautiful.

Ask yourself...

Where can I go to connect to nature?
Where can I take a walk and be in wonder of
the natural beauty around me?
Can I let my face be kissed by sunlight
or fresh air everyday?

September 7

Clear clutter

"Clear clutter.
Make space for you."
Magdalena Vandenberg

Today's message...

Having a clear mind and a clear space allows you to
think and act with more clarity and purpose.
If your space is cluttered and your mind
is jammed, you don't have room for
new wonderful things to enter your life.
Clear your space and mind.
Make room for new amazing things.
Let go of unhealthy food that clutters your body as well.

Ask yourself...

What can I do to protect my space?
What clutter do I need to release?
What energy is surrounding me in all my personal spaces?

September 6

Experience stillness

"Silence has a mysterious calming effect, allowing your soul to be at peace with your thoughts."
Anthony Douglas Williams

Remember...

Be still and locate your inner voice.
The peace you are looking for is already inside you.
Be still and know that you can access this calm.
You can only obtain peace from inside yourself;
you will not find it in the outer world.
Move past the bustle and chatter of life
and listen to your inner light
that guides you and feeds you.

Affirm...

I find inner peace in stillness.
I move past busy chaos and choose silence.
I listen to my inner voice.

September 5

Get some fresh air

"Sometimes, you need to step outside, get some fresh air, and remind yourself of who you are and who you want to be."
Unknown

Remember...

Walking is the way nature intended us
to move around and stay healthy.
Movement is essential for the body.
Movement can be like medicine,
in that it changes a person's physical,
emotional, and mental states.
Step away, go for a walk,
and look at life from
a different perspective.

Affirm...

I walk daily.
I enjoy fresh air and movement.
I gain new perspective and positive outlook.

September 4

Live well

***"Eat like you love yourself.
Move like you love yourself.
Speak like you love yourself.
Act like you love yourself."***
Tara Stiles

Remember...

Food choices that are healthy
and good for you make you feel
energized and alive.
Going for a walk is a wonderful way
to clear your head.
Make healthy choices to live well today.
You deserve it.

Ask yourself...

How can I move my body to help energize me?
What healthy foods can I eat?
How can I fuel my spirit and my body today?

September 3

Show up as your best self

"Believe and act as if it were impossible to fail."
Charles Kettering

Today's message...

Today, decide how you want to be
and show up in your life.
Make the effort to be
the person you desire to be.
Act as if you are already the best version of you,
and show up exactly the way you want to.
Think about the person you truly want to be.
Then make every effort today to be that person.

Ask yourself...

Who do I want to be today?
What is the best version of me?
How do I want to show up in my life today?

September 2

Make a change

"Only I can change my life.
No one can do it for me."
Carol Burnett

Ask yourself...

Can I change something I do on a daily basis?
How can I fall more in love with my decisions?
What do I believe in and will take a stand about?

Remember...

Every new day is a chance to
be courageous and make a change.
To move forward in life
you need to believe in yourself,
have conviction in your beliefs,
and the confidence to execute your convictions.
Success means to commit without any guarantee.

Affirm...

I am courageous.
I stand up for what I believe in.
I commit to my dreams on a daily basis.

September 1

Love yourself

"When I accept myself, I am freed from the burden of needing others to accept me."
Dr. Steve Maraboli

Today's message...

Other people do not determine
your self-worth, you are in charge.
Work on being in love with the person in the mirror.
Don't limit yourself because of what people might think.
Just be yourself,
and let people see the real, imperfect,
magical person that you are.

Affirm...

I am comfortable looking in the mirror and saying,
I love you.
I am worthy of loving.
I see love all around me.

August 31

Be proud of who you are

"Take pride in how far you have come.
Have faith I show far you can go.
But don't forget to enjoy the journey."
Michael Josephson

Today's message...

Don't wait until you've reached your goals
to be proud of yourself.
Make sure you are proud of every step
you take towards reaching your goal.
Do one thing today to make you
feel proud of yourself.

Ask yourself...

What am I most proud of?
Who am I when I am at my best?
How would my best friend describe me?

August 30

Take charge of your schedule

"If it's not useful or beautiful, it has no place in your life."
Kacy Paide

Today's message...

In order to change your life,
you need to change your priorities.
When you lack time, you are actually
lacking in your priorities.
Getting organized is a daily routine that
helps you finish projects that you have started.
It is the first important step
towards your larger goals.

Ask yourself...

What has the highest return for my future?
What stands between my dreams and me?
Can I take moments everyday to get more organized?

August 29

Be present and trust the future is taken care of

"It is in the compelling zest of high adventure and of victory, and in creative action, that man finds his supreme joys."
Antoine de Saint-Exupery

Today's message...

What feels like today's limits
will be tomorrow's victories.
Accept challenges so that you can feel
the power of being victorious.
Keep persevering and great
accomplishments will come to you.
Talk about your blessings more than
you talk about your problems.

Ask yourself...

What will help me realize how valuable I am?
Am I missing some blessings?
What would help me forget the days troubles
and focus on the good things?

August 28

View yourself positively

"My body isn't flawed,
my thinking is."
Stephanie Lahart

Today's message...

Change your thinking and you can change the way you see yourself and the world. If you think positive thoughts your life and perception of yourself will be positive. Monitor your thoughts.

Ask yourself...

What is the story I am telling myself about me?
What do I hold on to that I would be better off letting go?
What are some better feeling thoughts?

August 27

Self-Acceptance

"Dear you, make peace with the mirror and watch your reflection change."
Unknown

Today's message...

Embrace and love your body.
It's the most amazing thing that you will every own.
Take care of your health
and love your body for being able
to house your spirit.
Fall in love with taking care of yourself.

Affirm...

I love myself.
I am full of love and kindness.
I am beautiful.

August 26

Follow your joy

"If you're not excited about it,
it's not the right path."
Abraham Hicks

Today's Message...

It is very important to follow your own path.
Your journey is going to be unique and not a straight line.
There will be ups and downs. There are no footsteps
you can follow and no perfect map for you,
but you can follow your joy and excitement.
The energy you feel is a good indication of the
correct path for you at any given moment.
When you follow your own excitement,
motivation, drive, and focus will be almost effortless.
Instead of struggling and getting stressed
about your future or correct path,
follow what brings you excitement!

Ask Yourself...

What excites me?
What brings me joy?
What am I drawn towards?

August 25

Life is about choices

"Every day brings new choices."
Martha Beck

Today's message...

When something bad happens you have choices:
you can either let it define you, destroy you,
or you can let it strengthen you.
Your choices determine you character.

Affirm...

I am not what happened to me.
I am what I choose to become.
Experiences make me stronger.

August 24

Practice self-control

"You can do anything,
but not everything."
David Allen

Remember...

Self-control is the ability to
prevent yourself from making bad choices.
Discipline your mind to remember
what you desire in your life.
The cost of self-control is less than
the cost of lack of discipline.
You can achieve great things
with self-discipline.

Affirm...

I am in control of my life.
I make good choices.
Self-discipline and self-control make my life better.

August 23

Work on you

"When you are living the best version of yourself you inspire others."

Dr. Steve Maraboli

Today's message...

Make yourself a priority and focus on
making yourself better each day.
Each day is an opportunity to be
a better version of yourself.
Your life only gets better
when you work on yourself.

Ask yourself...

How can I love myself more today?
What can I be grateful for right now?
How can I be a better person today?

August 22

Enjoy the moment

"Sometimes what you're looking for comes when you're not looking at all."
Old Saying

Today's message...

Life is full of surprises and unexpected gifts.
Life is a gift, so never forget to
have fun and enjoy every moment.
The more grateful you are for your life,
the more gifts will show up for you.
Your life, challenges and all,
is a beautiful gift filled with opportunities.

Ask yourself...

How can I be thankful for what I have?
What needs of mine are being met on a regular basis?
What gifts and opportunities, big or small,
have surrounded me?

August 21

Big transformations revitalize you

***"Don't be afraid of change,
it is leading you to a new beginning."***
Joyce Meyer

Today's message...

Change can seem scary if you focus on
what you have to give up,
but change is exciting when you think about
what you will gain.
When things are not going well in your life,
find a new path that will lead you in a new direction.
Change over time in your life is inevitable
but you transforming is a personal choice.

Affirm...

I embrace change.
I am capable.
I am confident.

August 20

See beauty

"***Everything has beauty, but not everyone sees it.***"
Confucius

Today's message...

Everything has beauty,
but we don't always notice
or see it around us.
Take the time to notice
all the beauty around you
and within you.
How you feel about
yourself and the world
is much more important
than how you look.

Affirm...

I see beauty and light within me.
I am beautiful.
I notice the beauty around me.

August 19

Stand in your light

"Keep your head high no matter what happens. You'll be alright. If the moment hurts, do not fall victim to its pain. Look Ahead. Focus on what can be. Focus on dreams. You'll make it."

Unknown

Remember...

Hold your head up and feel proud,
you deserve to shine.
Be proud of your mini accomplishments
along the way to reaching your goal.
Continue to believe in yourself and stand tall.
Your success can be peace of mind
that you know you did your best.
You did it, you have come this far, be proud.

Affirm...

I am successful.
I am surrounded by victory.
I am proud of my accomplishments.

August 18

Make your own joy

***"So plant your own garden
and decorate your own soul,
instead of waiting for someone
to bring you flowers."***
Jorge Luis Borges

Today's message...

Do more of what brings you joy and happiness.
Tap into the things that bring you joy.
Take walks in nature
and do things that help you reflect
on what brings you joy.

Ask yourself...

How can I bring more joy and happiness into my life?
What is in the way of my happiness today?
How can I live the highest, truest expression of myself?

August 17

Imagine what is possible

"It is what it is.
It was what it was.
It will be what it will be.
Don't stress* It.*"
Unknown

Remember…

Don't be afraid to try something new,
when you do you can only grow.
Don't stress, keep imagining what is possible for you.
Do the things you love without any doubt.
Don't be afraid to change,
it will lead you to new beginnings and opportunities.
Be curious, try new things, and ask questions.

Affirm…

I take risk and enjoy the rewards.
I remain curious and intrigued in my life.
I imagine great possibilities for me.

August 16

Be happy for others

"Admire other people's beauty and talent without questioning your own."
Brooke Hampton

Today's message...

Don't compare yourself with
anyone else in this world.
Only compare yourself to
the self you were yesterday.

Ask yourself...

What is it about others that I can be honestly happy for?
How can I stop comparing myself to others?
When good things happen to others,
how can I be enthusiastic for them?

August 15

Notice beautiful things

"Life is a series of thousands of tiny miracles. Notice them."
Unknown

Today's message...

Beauty is all around you,
so take the time to notice
and enjoy the magnificence.

Ask yourself...

What is beautiful in my life?
If I were to be an outsider dropped into my life,
what would they find beautiful and amazing?

Remember...

Beauty is all around you.
Take time to open your eyes,
and you will notice and experience
more beauty.

August 14

Turn lemons into lemonade

"Imagination will take you everywhere."
Albert Einstein

Today's message...

You create your own reality with
your thoughts, feelings, and attitude.
The past is where you learned lessons,
be grateful for your life,
and apply your lessons to your future.
Sometimes you need those days that are bad,
in order to truly appreciate the days that are good.

Ask yourself...

How can I refocus on where I want to go?
Can I think of a time that I made the best of my situation?
How has the past made me better today?

August 13

Perfect isn't real

"Beauty is the opposite of perfection.
It's confidence, charisma, and character."
Unknown

Today's message...

Being happy does not mean that everything is perfect;
it means that you've decided to look
beyond the imperfections.
Perfection is an unattainable goal.
There is nothing more beautiful than
a person being unapologetically themselves,
comfortable in their own perfect imperfections.

Ask yourself...

How can I be the perfectly imperfect person I want to be?
What is my own real beauty?
Are my goals realistic and attainable?

August 12

Take a negativity diet

"Protect your enthusiasm from the negativity of others."
H. Jackson Brown, Jr.

Today's message...

Take a negativity diet.
Don't participate in any negative
focus, talk, or thinking.
Shift away from it as fast as you can
and notice how much better your feel.
Negativity is the thief of joy and enthusiasm.

Affirm...

I free myself from negative thinking.
I speak kindly to others and myself.
I let go of negative thoughts and move to gratitude.

August 11

Everything is blossoming

"Be like the lotus:
trust in the light,
grow through the dirt,
believe in new beginnings."
Unknown

Remember...

Do what you love and surround yourself
with beautiful people and things.
Be who you were meant to be, and blossom.
If you desire love and abundance in your life,
you have to be willing to
give away love and abundance.

Affirm...

I am open to receiving.
I prosper and flourish.
I am surrounded by love and abundance.

August 10

Spread kindness

"Kindness makes you
the most beautiful person in the world
no matter what you look like."
Old Saying

Today's message...

Kindness can help people that
you didn't even know needed your help.
Be that person who makes people smile a little bigger.

Ask yourself...

Who might need my kindness today?
When was I really kind and how did it feel?
What are some ways that I can practice kindness?

August 9

Appreciate those you love

***"Family: like branches on a tree;
we all grow in different directions
yet our roots remain as one."***
Old Saying

Today's message...

Your roots are what have made you who you are
and what you have become.
Always take note of who supports you genuinely.
These are the people who make up your family.
You will find peace when you surround yourself
with caring kind people.
Never confuse people who are always around
with the people that are always there for you.

Ask yourself...

What people invest in me?
Who are the supportive people who can help me
achieve my goals, and love me without condition?
Can I find ways to deeply appreciate
the people around me who love me?

August 8

Pay attention to your inner experience

"The best cure for stress and worry is a quiet mind."
Napoleon Bonaparte

Remember...

Stand in your own truth and you will walk along a path of happiness. Make sure you listen to your own voice and be an original. Be yourself no matter what other people think. If something is really important to you, find a way to make it happen.

Affirm...

I become what inspires me.
I know my truth and what's important to me.
I follow signs and guidance.

August 7

Be impeccable

***"Never bend your head.
Always hold it high.
Look the world straight in the eye."***
Helen Keller

Today's message...

Act with certainty, confidence, and positivity.
Let go of doubt and hostility.
Now is the time to act without hesitation.
Every little bit of effort makes movement
towards your goals, no matter how big or small.
You were born with the ability to
be amazing and impeccable.

Ask yourself...

How can I step things up a notch, and gather discipline?
What action can I take to reach my dreams?
If my plan A doesn't work, what is my next plan?

August 6

Notice energy

"No one can make you feel inferior without your consent."
Eleanor Roosevelt

Today's message...

Think positive thoughts today
and notice how your whole day
will feel energized.
Eat healthy and drink water
to feel nourished and healthy today.
Choose to be optimistic today.
It will boost your energy.
Be responsible for the energy
you bring today.

Affirm...

I feel glorious.
I am energetic.
I feel alive.

August 5

Set sail on new waters

"Sometimes good things fall apart
so better things can fall together."
Marilyn Monroe

Today's message...

It's time to wipe the slate clean and focus forward.
Sometimes you have to let go of things in order to
make room for new things to come into your life.
You have a clean slate every day you wake up.
You have a chance to change every day.
The end of something means
there is a new beginning.

Ask yourself...

What in my life needs a fresh start?
What lessons have I learned from my life so far?
What new beginning or new story do I want to write?

August 4

Spread Happiness

"Be the reason someone smiles today."
Old Saying

Today's message...

Compliment people.
Take time to magnify their strengths,
not their weaknesses.
Use every opportunity to be
grateful for others
and express your appreciation
and kindness to others.

Ask yourself...

How can I make others smile?
What actions do I make that
contribute to others' happiness?
Who needs my appreciation today?

August 3

Look for good

"You gotta look for the good in the bad,
the happy in the sad,
the gain in your pain,
and what makes you grateful not hateful."
Karen Salmansohn

Today's message...

I've found that no matter how seemingly horrible
a circumstance may appear,
I can always find some good in it.
Ask yourself, how has this happened FOR me?

Ask yourself...

What good is here that I presently cannot see?
What is the blessing in disguise?
What is this situation telling me?

August 2

Don't worry what people think

"What you think of yourself is much more important than what people think of you."
Seneca the Elder

Today's message...

Most of the time when we are interpreting
what others are thinking
we may not be totally accurate.
It's impossible to actually know
what other people think.
Worrying about others opinions is
very draining and may not be accurate.

Affirm...

I choose not to read into situations.
I focus on my own self.
I only concern myself with thinking
positive thoughts about myself.

August 1

Choose calm

"Anger is a sign that something needs to change."
Mark Epstein

Today's Message...

Anger is a funny thing: it builds really fast and it turns off the part of our brain that can think rationally.
Slow down, take a deep breath, and understand that anger is a message.
What is it telling you?
What needs to change?
Energy is everything.
Be careful when you spend your energy.
Anger is a natural defence against pain in your life, don't waste your energy being in anger.
Use this time to calm down, reflect, and make change.
Find your zen place.

Affirm...

I am human.
I am safe.
My anger is a signal.

July 31

Be resilient

"Resilience means you experience,
you feel, you fail, you hurt.
You fall, but you keep going."
Andrew Zolli

Today's message...

Resilience is accepting your new reality,
even if it is less good than the one you had before.
Adversity and suffering are part of life's teaching moments.
Through them we become more resilient.

Affirm...

I am resilient and able to bounce back.
I am strong.
I have skills to help me through anything.

July 30

Look up

"You'll never find a rainbow
if you're looking down."
Charlie Chaplin

Today's message...

Lift your head when you're down.
You have to fight through some bad days
to earn the best days.

Affirm...

I keep looking up.
I smile and look up at endless possibilities.
I keep my head up and think positive.

July 29

Respect your feelings as messages

"Respect yourself enough to walk away from anything that no longer serves you, grows you, or makes you happy."
Robert Tew

Today's message...

Remain sensitive to parts of your life that don't make you feel good and try to remove those aspects.
Pay attention to your gut feelings,
no matter good or bad.
Limit your time with negative toxic people.
Sometimes you have to give up on
certain people in your life,
it simply isn't worth the struggle.
Letting go of toxic people is a form of
honouring and respecting yourself.

Ask yourself...

What aspects of my life do not feel right?
How can I protect my spirit from contaminated situations and people?
What people in my life raise me up?

July 28

Time to celebrate

"The more you praise and celebrate your life, the more there is in life to celebrate."
Oprah Winfrey

Today's message...

When you are grateful for all the things in your life,
fear disappears and abundance appears.
Be happy and express gratitude.
It will open the door to abundance in your life.
Your abundant attitude is like a magnet that will
draw positive things and people to you.

Remember...

Life isn't always perfect, but it's always
what you make of it.
Good times, crazy friends, and family
make the best memories.
When life is sweet, be thankful and celebrate.
When life is harsh, be thankful and grow from it.

July 27

One step at a time

"A journey of a thousand miles begins with a single step."
Lao-Tzu

Today's message...

They say don't compare someone else's
middle or end to your start.
Start with one step, however small
that first step might be.
You have to start somewhere.

Affirm...

I keep going.
Today I am one step closer than I was yesterday.
I continue to make progress.

July 26

Meditate

"The quieter you become,
the more you can hear."
Baba Ram Dass

Remember...

The more you meditate or reflect
and spend time out in nature,
you will raise your ability to get in touch
with your inner voice.
Train your mind to say and think good things
as often as possible.
Don't listen to people who tell you what to do,
but rather list to the people who
encourage and inspire you.

Affirm...

I listen to my inner voice.
I pay close attention to my thoughts.
I choose to hear positive messages.

July 25

Be silent

"Silence isn't empty.
It's full of answers."
Lori Deschene

Today's message...

Be still. Empty yourself of the mental chatter and the busyness of life to create a state of mindfulness and awareness. There is healing in stillness. The quieter your mind, the more you hear your inner voice. Inner peace comes when you don't let other people or events control your emotions and thinking.

Ask yourself...

If I could choose my thoughts more carefully, what would I choose?
How can I keep what brings me peace, and release what brings me tension?
Is there something I can let go today?

July 24

Fix what is broken

"Make peace with your broken pieces."
Unknown

Today's message...

When something is broken you try to fix it.
See your life in the same way.
When you feel broken, fix yourself.
If you don't know how,
take time to learn and figure it out.
Remember that sometimes
good things fall apart to make
room for something better.

Ask yourself...

What needs my attention?
When I feel I'm falling apart,
what helps me get back together?
What can I do to make me feel good today?

July 23

Be happy for others

"She is beautiful but so am I."
Unknown

Today's Message...

If you get a feeling of jealousy, simply shift your perception. Consider jealousy an expression of what you want more in your life. If you feel jealous look very closely at your own insecurities and be open and honest about what you desire for yourself. You will feel empowered and more at peace when you look at that feeling of jealousy in this new way. Face your own fears that might be holding you back from great things. Be your own person and make great things happen in your own life.

Affirm...

I use jealous feelings as inspiration.
I allow my feelings to make me better.
I am happy for others and myself.

Ask Yourself...

What makes me jealous?
What do I need more of in my life?
How can I use this information to benefit me?

July 22

Shine bright

"Choose to shine."
Old Saying

Today's message...

Don't let anyone or anything
dim your sparkle.
Remember who you are
and the light that you
bring to this world.
Choose to make everything
around you beautiful.
Create a beautiful day!

Affirm...

I shine bright.
I am a ray of sunshine.
I continue to sparkle.

July 21

Be grateful

"The struggle ends when gratitude begins."
Neale Donald Walsh

Today's message...

If you're experiencing any
level of pain or discomfort,
the easiest way to shift out of it
is to ask yourself what
you're grateful to have.
At times our own light
goes dim and we feel down;
use the power of gratitude
to help make you shine again.

Ask yourself...

What am I grateful for?
What are my strengths?
What makes my life good?

July 20

Go for a walk

"Thoughts come clearly while one walks."
Thomas Mann

Today's message...

Habituate yourself to walk every day.
You are the most important person in your life
and deserve to be taken care of.
Make time for movement to increase
vitality and gain perspective.
When you free your body, you free your mind.
Science shows us that walking improves circulation
and oxygenates your entire body, mind, and spirit.

Ask yourself...

Life is a balance between rest and movement;
am I getting enough of both?
When can I step away and take a walk?
What clears my mental clutter?

July 19

Speak kind towards yourself

"You will never speak to anyone more than you speak to yourself in your head, be kind to yourself."
Unknown

Ask yourself...

Am I hiding my greatness behind past guilt?
Can I inhale the future and exhale the past?
What lessons keep getting presented to me and what can I learn from these situations?

Remember...

Forgive and let go of the past so you control your happiness.
If you remove the guilt and make a commitment to yourself to learn from and do better in future situations, you take back your control.
Focus on your positive attributes and don't be so hard on yourself.

Affirm...

I let go of guilt.
I forgive and focus forward.
I speak kindly to myself.

July 18

Connect with yourself

"The thing about truth is that
it exists beyond belief.
It is true even if nobody believes it."
Dieter F. Uchtdorf

Today's message...

Success is about living your life according to
your own truth, what is important to you.
Be bold and be yourself,
not what people expect you to be.
You can learn a lot about yourself if you
pay attention to your life, and truth will reveal itself.
You define what is important to you by deciding
what you spend your time doing.

Ask yourself...

How arm I genuine and original?
Who am I meant to be, and how can I fully be myself?
Am I paying attention to what inspires me in my life?

July 17

Expect great things

"You must expect great things of yourself before you can do them."
Michael Jordan

Today's message...

Believe in yourself and expect great things;
if you don't, you just might end up being right.
Take the initiative to think about what
great things could happen for you, what wonderful
opportunities might be in store for you.
Set some really fantastic dreams in place
and then expect those things to show up for you.
This expectation and faith will build up your
strength, confidence, and motivation.

Ask yourself...

What do I want most for myself?
What is my desired outcome for the day?
What would make my day great?

July 16

Value your life and be present

"There is so much peace in the present moment."
Unknown

Remember...

Your mind is a very powerful tool that you can use to fill with positive thoughts. Gratitude can transform your world from ordinary to a life of beauty and opportunities. Be sure to be thankful and cherish each day as a gift. Notice the tiny miracles all around you, even when you are thinking about your future dreams.

Affirm...

There is joy in my life.
I have an extraordinary life.
I value all the good things around me today.

July 15

Be grateful

"When you arise in the morning,
think of what a precious privilege
it is to be alive -
to breathe, to think, to enjoy, to love."
Marcus Aurelius

Today's message...

Take every opportunity to marvel
in all the good things in your life.
When you focus on what is good
and what you are grateful for in your life,
it makes your world seem better.
Pay attention to all the great people, the good
situations, and everything that makes you smile.
Put lots of attention and energy into the good things.
Being grateful brings a sense of joy and peace.

Affirm...

I am surrounded by love.
I am thankful for all the blessings around me.
So many things work well for me.

July 14

Focus on you

"Jealousy is just love and hate at the same time."
Drake

Remember...

Jealous is simply a lack of self-confidence.
When you catch yourself feeling jealous,
think of ways you can improve your confidence.
Do things that work on you.

Ask yourself...

Why am I jealous of this person?
What can I do to make myself feel better?
How can I notice my strengths instead of others'?

July 13

Life feels good inside

"Find a place inside where there's joy."
Joseph Campbell

Today's message...

Create a life that feels really good on the inside, not just that it looks good on the outside to others. Real beauty comes from the inside out.

Ask yourself...

What makes me joyful?
What do I want to bring into my life?
What makes me proud of who I am?

July 12

Thoughts create feelings

***"Thoughts are powerful,
and what we think and feel
is what we create."***
Dr. Bradley Nelson

Today's message...

Positive thoughts generate positive feelings
and positive results in your life.
Your thinking and the stories that you tell yourself
create your feelings.
If you want to change your feelings,
you can change your thoughts.

Affirm...

I am in charge of my feelings.
I choose good feeling thoughts.
I focus on positive feeling thinking.

July 11

Choice

***"I am NOT a product of my circumstances.
I am a product of my decisions."***
Steven Covey

Today's message...

Your current life is made up from the
choices you have made up until today.
Your life is a constant stream of choices.
It is important to keep making good choices and decisions.
You create the world you live in with your choices.
Make them good!!

Ask yourself...

What are the possibilities?
What good decisions can I make today?
What are my choices?

July 10

Making decisions

"Every decision I make
is the right one for me."
Louise Hay

Today's message...

Will this give me energy or deplete my energy?
When you're having a tough time deciding
something, ask yourself this question,
and make a conscious choice from there.
Then once you have made a decision,
know that you have made
the right decision for you, yourself.

Ask yourself...

What is the best outcome for me?
How will that decision make me feel?
Am I considering all options?

July 9

Everything will be ok

"What defines us is how well we rise after we fall."
Zig Ziglar

Today's message...

Pick yourself up and dry your eyes,
everything will be okay.
There is no such thing as failing;
everything is an opportunity to learn.

Affirm...

I can get through challenges.
I will be ok.
I can bounce back.

July 8

Think, feel, and imagine good things

***"What you think, you become.
What you feel, you attract.
What you imagine, you create."***
Gautama Buddha

Today's message...

Take notice of your thoughts.
Your thinking and imagination are powerful tools you can use to bring good things into your life.
Think thoughts that have a good feeling around them.

Ask yourself...

What good feeling thoughts can I think?
What good feelings can I experience?
How can I use my imagination to create a good life for myself?

July 7

Create your own happy

"Don't let your happiness depend on something you may lose."
C.S. Lewis

Today's message...

You create your own happiness inside yourself. Things outside of you do not determine your happiness. Avoid putting the keys to your happiness in someone else's pocket.
Take back your power.

Affirm...

I am in charge of my happiness.
I focus on my needs.
I am happy.

July 6

Take a break

"Sometimes you gotta take a break from all the noise to appreciate the beauty of silence."
Robert Tew

Remember...

Just because your childhood is over,
does not mean that your playtime is over.
Play can make you stronger
and develops your ability to
laugh and see humour in life.
Change the way that you see things
so that you can gain perspective.
Take a break today!

Affirm...

I regain perspective.
I make time for play and laughter.
My joy creates miracles.

July 5

Do what is important to you

***"If it's important, you'll find a way.
If it's not, you'll find an excuse."***
Ryan Blair

Today's message...

It is less about having time,
and more about making time,
for what is important to you.
Prioritize what matters most to you.
You define what is important to you
by what you dedicate your time to.

Ask yourself...

What is the highest and best use of my time?
What matters most to me?
How can I be clear and prioritize what is
most important to me?

July 4

Enjoy others' beauty

"Just because you don't look like somebody who you think is attractive doesn't mean you aren't attractive. Flowers are lovely, but so are sunsets, and they look nothing alike."

Unknown

Remember...

Beauty is a funny thing.
Others can be beautiful in a completely different way than you. Never let their beauty make you feel less than or inferior.
Be happy for others' beauty,
and embrace the gift that they are.
Continue to love your own beauty as well.

Affirm...

I am beautiful.
I am unique.
I share in others' happiness.

July 3

Don't compare yourself to others

"Learn from everyone but compare yourself to no one."
Brooke Hampton

Today's message...

Stop yourself from comparing yourself to others.
Try to simply see others as inspiration,
not a measure of comparison, as it will
deplete you and waste your energy.
Focus instead on how you can
keep getting better yourself.

Ask Yourself...

What do I want for myself?
What would make me feel good about myself?
What is best for me right now?